An introduction to
STAINED AND DECORATIVE
GLASS

An introduction to
STAINED AND DECORATIVE
GLASS

Oriel Hicks

D&S
BOOKS

First published in 2001 by D&S Books

© 2001 D&S Books

D&S Books
Cottage Meadow, Bocombe,
Parkham, Bideford
Devon, England
EX39 5PH

e-mail us at:-
enquiries.dspublishing@care4free.net

This edition printed 2001

ISBN 1-903327-12-1

Editorial Director: Sarah King
Editor: Clare Haworth-Maden
Project Editor: Judith Millidge
Designer: 2H Design

Distributed in the UK & Ireland by
Bookmart Limited
Desford Road
Enderby
Leicester LE9 5AD

Distributed in Australia by
Herron Books
39 Commercial Road
Fortitude Valley
Queensland 4006

1 3 5 7 9 10 8 6 4 2

Contents

Introduction

It is not known exactly when glassmaking first started, but it was almost certainly at least four thousand years ago. The technique was probably invented accidentally by the Egyptians or the Phoenicians, when firing clay pots in the sand; glass beads would form from the silica and other chemicals around it in the sand. Glass was then regarded as a very precious commodity, on a par with gold.

It was another two thousand years at least, in about the first century BC, that a method of glassblowing was invented along the eastern Mediterranean coast, and eventually the Romans were able to make the highly prized sheet glass, which was sometimes used in their houses. The glass was rarely completely clear, and the glassblowers soon realised that the colour of glass produced depended on what kind of wood was used in the furnace, because the chemical composition of the different types of potash varied. They then began to experiment, adding oxides of different metals and other chemicals to create different hues and depths of colour.

Star of the Sea, St. Mary's Catholic Church, Isles of Scilly.
Designed and made by the author.

Stained-glass windows

The oldest extant stained-glass window is in Augsburg, Germany, and dates from about AD 1000. Windows were probably being made in various parts of Europe for at least a century before this, however. Stained glass was used in churches to illustrate stories from the Bible at a time when most of the congregation was illiterate. Some of the finest, and most famous, stained glass is in the cathedral of Chartres in France, which was made during the twelfth and thirteenth centuries. Stained glass became very popular all over Europe, and most cathedrals and churches, right down to the smallest, had some stained glass in them.

Tragically, during the seventeenth-century in England, much of this beautiful glass was ripped out and destroyed because it was considered idolatrous. The windows dating from before that time that are still in existence are those that monks had the foresight to remove and hide in crypts or graveyards until it was safe to reinstate them. Because stained glass was used solely for churches, its production subsequently ceased, and the recipes for many of colours were lost forever. By the end of the seventeenth century, a new kind of glass had become popular in churches. It was not stained, but clear glass that had been painted with coloured enamels and then fired. Although the technique was permanent, the colour was superficial and didn't have the depth and vibrancy of stained glass.

This technique continued to be used until the later part of the nineteenth century, when William Morris, a founding member of the Arts and Crafts Movement, along with the artists and designers Dante Gabriel Rossetti and Edward Burne-Jones, demanded the making of real stained glass for their windows. At around this time, too, the native New Yorke, Louis Comfort Tiffany, was working with stained glass in the United States. Since white was added to it to make it semi-opalescent, the glass that he used was not as transparent. This type of glass, which is still made today, is usually called Tiffany glass. With its soft, flowing lines and romantic subjects, the style of these artists' stained glass was typical of the time.

St. Christopher & St. Mary's, Church of England Church, Isles of Scilly.

Stained Glass window in author's house.

Dalles de verre

During the two world wars of the twentieth century, many churches and cathedrals were either destroyed or had their windows blown out. The glass in the windows of some modern churches and cathedrals is often a new type of glass called *dalles de verre*, which requires a completely different method of creation. Instead of being blown into sheets, molten glass is poured into moulds to form small slabs about 2.5 centimetres (1 inch) thick. When cold, these slabs are removed from their moulds and chipped to size and shape with a chisel-edged hammer so that the edges are faceted. The design must be kept very simple, mainly using coloured squares, triangles and oblongs. The coloured glass for each section of the design is laid out on the floor on a bed of sand and reinforced resin or concrete is then poured between the slabs of glass and left to set. The large section thus formed is used as a building block, which, with other blocks, forms a window that acts as a wall. The crown of Liverpool Cathedral was made in this way, as was the beautiful window at Buckfast Abbey in Devon, where there is still a workshop run by monks who design and make this kind of stained-glass window.

As occurred during the nineteenth century, the end of the twentieth century saw a big revival in the popularity of stained glass, which is now commonly used in public buildings like libraries and courts and in the offices of multinational companies. Today it is also a popular craft that is practised by many people.

Different view of the stained glass window.

CHAPTER 1
Materials and equipment

Glass is made by melting silica (sand) with potash and soda at a temperature of about 1,300°C (2,372°F). In true stained glass, the colour is added at this stage by mixing in various oxides of metals and rare earths. Copper oxide will give you green glass, for example, while cobalt oxide will give you blue and antimony results in various shades of red and deep amber. The most expensive colour is cranberry pink, which is made by adding small quantities of 9 carat gold and copper to obtain the beautiful pink colour.

Today, stained glass can be made either by the original method of blowing glass, when it is called antique glass, or by a machine process. In both cases, the colour is added in the same way by using oxides.

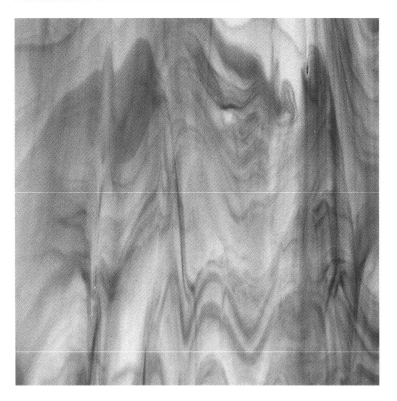

Opalescent blue/green glass.

Types of glass

In the mouth-blown, antique method, a ball of molten glass is taken from the crucible and blown into a cylinder, called a muff. This is cooled and the cylinder is then cut down one side, reheated and opened out to form a flat sheet. It has striations, reams and bubbles in it, which give it movement and life. It is often not completely flat, and because the thickness varies across the sheet, the depth of colour changes. This type of glass, which is called a pot colour, as the colour is added in the crucible, is used in church windows and restoration work. Sometimes two or more colours are used in the same sheet of glass; this is called reamy. Another type of antique glass is called flash glass, which is made by using clear glass and 'flashing' molten glass of a different colour onto one surface. This is used for cut or acid-etched glass, where the coloured layer is removed with either a grinding wheel or hydrofluoric acid. The Victorians used a lot of this type of glass in their doors and windows.

Glass can also be poured onto a bed of sand and rolled flat. This gives it definite 'right' and 'wrong' sides, as one surface will pick up the texture of the sand. Machine-made glass is poured between two rollers, one of which may be slightly textured to give the glass an obscured finish.

Tiffany glass is made by adding small amounts of white glass to coloured glass, which results in a slight wispy appearance and brings out the colour without the need for backlighting. If more white is added, the finished sheet will be more opalescent, which means that although nothing is visible through it, light will still penetrate the glass, making it glow. Tiffany glass is therefore useful for lampshades, clock faces and photo frames, in other words, objects that are intended to be looked at rather than through. The layers of white in the coloured glass can be seen on the cut edge of the sheet, rather like the lettering that runs through seaside rock. Another type of opalescent glass is iridescent glass. This is made by taking a sheet of coloured opalescent glass and painting one side with a lustre. The glass is then fired at a lower temperature than that at which the glass melts, making the lustre permanent and giving the glass the attractive appearance of mother of pearl or oil on water.

Interestingly, glass is technically a viscous, not a solid, substance. If a sheet of glass is left in an upright position in a church window for centuries, for example, it will become thicker at the lower edge than at the upper, because gravity has caused the glass to flow downwards. Also, if a sheet of glass is scored but not broken, the score line will eventually close, or heal, over. Although it remains visible, it will not subsequently break along this line.

Iridescent glass.

Glass paints

The glass paints referred to here are not the traditional types found on church windows, which are only used for shading real stained glass to give the details of faces, hands and robes, for inscriptions and so on. The paints that have been used for the projects in this book are instead coloured lacquers that are applied to one surface of a sheet of clear glass and are then left to dry through exposure to the air rather than fired in a kiln.

These paints can be bought at art and craft shops and are sold in a range of colours. Their base can be either water, white spirit or cellulose thinners, the latter being the most highly toxic, but also the most colour-fast (the others tend to fade in strong sunlight after a year or two). An outline relief is used to contain the glass paint in their different areas of colour. This is a type of black, gold or silver acrylic paste that is sold in a tube with a long nozzle. After application, it is left to dry for a couple of hours before the glass paint is used.

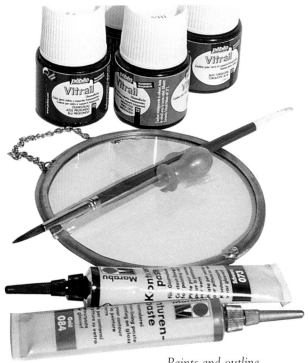

Paints and outline.

Etching paste

Although a type of opalescent white glass paint applied to glass will give the appearance of an etched texture, true etching on glass is always done using an etching paste containing hydrofluoric acid. This will etch only about 8 microns into the glass and will therefore not affect the strength of toughened glass (an important consideration if it is to be used for a panel in a door, for instance).

Hydrofluoric acid is a very dangerous substance and must be used with great care. It is imperative that rubber gloves are worn at all times and that work is carried out either in a very well ventilated area or preferably outside. Brushes and tools used for etching should, for the sake of safety, not be used for any other purpose.

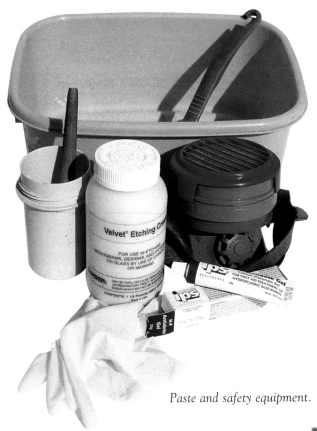

Paste and safety equipment.

Glasscutters

Various glass cutters and a jar of white spirit with sponge.

The earliest windows were cut using a hot metal rod to crack the glass by means of differential expansion, in the same way that plunging a hot wine glass into cold water will break it. Very intricate shapes could be cut in this way, usually by the monks who made the windows, but it was an extremely time-consuming method. Later, when it was discovered that a diamond was harder than glass, the glass was scored with this stone, breaking the surface tension. The glass was then cracked by the application of force underneath the cut.

Nowadays, a wheeled cutter made of steel or tungsten carbide is usually used to create the score line. Although a tungsten-carbide cutter is considerably more expensive than a steel cutter, it

is a good investment because a lot less pressure is needed to make the score line and the wheel will also last much longer. A pistol-grip tungsten cutter is also available, which is useful if you do not have enough strength in your hands to use a traditional cutter. Cutters are lubricated by means of white spirit or a thin machine oil within the shaft, which keeps the cutting wheel permanently oiled through a wick or gravity feed. If a steel-wheeled cutter, or one without a reservoir, is used, the wheel must always be lubricated with thin oil before a score line is made in the glass. For this purpose, it is a good idea to have a small jar to hand containing a piece of sponge soaked in white spirit to wipe away excess oil.

Different sized pairs of breaking pliers, straightedge and carborundum stone.

Other tools used in glasscutting

It is sometimes necessary to cut a long, straight line across a sheet of glass. This is more easily achieved with the use of a straight edge, when you would place the cutter against the top edge and then pull it towards you. The straight edge should have a non-slip strip on the underside and must be thick enough to ensure that the glasscutter does not jump onto it, instead remaining alongside it while you are cutting.

Cut-run pliers, which are a bit like tilebreakers, can be useful if you are a nervous of breaking the glass. They do exactly as their name indicates and replace the hands when breaking glass by gripping it on each side of the score line and applying pressure underneath it, causing the glass to break cleanly.

If you are confident enough to break the glass with your hands, however, when cutting a very narrow piece of glass it will still be necessary to hold it with a pair of breaking pliers in order to get a sufficient grip. Breaking pliers are wide-nosed pliers that meet only at their tips, which means that the glass is not damaged as they close. The straight end of the pliers is used to grip the glass parallel to the score line at the near edge of the cut, bending and thus breaking the glass much as a finger and thumb would.

Copper foil

Originally, only lead came was used for making window panels. Nowadays, however, it is more common to use copper foil for small, indoor panels and giftware. The foil, which comes on a reel, is available in different widths. One side is adhesive, enabling it to stick to the glass, and this adhesive side is covered in backing paper so that it runs off the reel more easily. The foil can either be backed with a transparent adhesive, or, if it is to be used with clear glass (in a terrarium, for instance) with black adhesive, which will prevent the copper colour being visible; silver-backed foil can be used on mirrored glass for the same reason.

Copper foil.

Foil accessories.

Accessories for foilwork

Although foil can be applied directly to the glass edge by hand, this is a fiddly process. It is much easier to use a handfoiler, which centres the copper foil on the edge of the glass and removes the backing paper as it goes along.

More intricate foiling tools are also available, which often work well with large pieces of glass, but not so efficiently with small ones. Some also crimp the foil around the piece of glass. If you are using a handfoiler, you could also invest in a separate tool called a handcrimper, but your fingers are often just as efficient.

Copper foil is put around the glass in order to take solder and is not actually seen on the finished object. Before solder is applied to the foil, however, the foil must be fluxed. Flux is an oil, and if the foil does not adhere to the glass thoroughly, the flux will seep underneath it and lift it off. Once the copper foil has been crimped to the glass edge, it must therefore be pressed down firmly with a small tool called a fid.

As well as being an oil, flux is acidic. Its main function is to deoxidise the copper foil prior to soldering and to make the solder flow. Because the flux burns away once the soldering iron is applied, a fume trap, which draws the fumes away from the area being soldered, is a highly recommended piece of equipment. You could also use small fan, but this is more likely to cool the soldering iron.

A fume trap.

Lead came

Lead is a soft substance, which will bend around very tight curves if necessary. It has been used to join pieces of glass together for as long as stained-glass windows have been made. It comes in lengths of approximately 2 metres (6 ½ feet) and in various widths. It is 'H'-shaped in section, with a channel on each side to take the pieces of glass. The crosspiece of the 'H'-section is called the heart, and the top and bottom, which are the parts seen when looking at a window, are each called the leaf.

When it is first cut, lead is a very shiny metal, but it soon oxidises to become a dull grey colour and continues to oxidise right the way through the lead, which is why many cathedrals have a stained-glass workshop on the premises to restore their windows (unless it is broken, the glass will last almost indefinitely, but, depending on the quality of the air in the location, the windows have to be removed, taken apart and the lead replaced every fifty to a hundred years).

Lead is so soft that it will rub off on your hands. Because it is a poisonous substance that can be absorbed through the skin and, when soldering, through inhalation, it is advisable to wear rubber gloves or a good barrier cream when using lead came and a mask when rubbing it down with a wire brush prior to soldering.

Lead came.

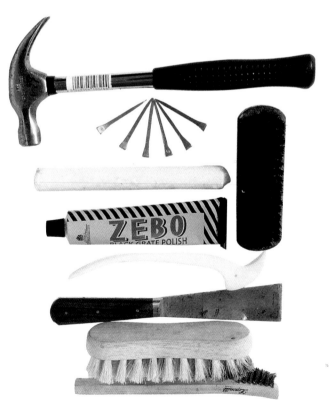

Lead working tools.

Tools for leadwork

The lead came should be cut with a sharp lead knife. Being a metal, the lead will blunt even the sharpest knife fairly quickly, so an oilstone is useful to keep the edge on it.

Because lead is such a soft substance, it often becomes damaged in transit and must then be straightened before use. To do this, one end of the lead came is gripped in a lead vice or cleat attached to a workbench, while the other is held with a pair of pliers, enabling the lead to be stretched for quite a distance. This process not only straightens the lead, but makes it stiffer and easier to work with.

If there are crimps in the lead, or the channel is not wide enough to take the piece of glass, the channel can be widened using either a fid or a tool designed to do a number of different tasks, perhaps unsurprisingly called a Nova all-purpose tool. Some people use a tool called a lathekin instead, or else an oyster knife, but these can be difficult to obtain. You could always make your own, however, or adapt a similar tool.

The grinder

Although a grinder is probably the most expensive piece of equipment that you will have to buy, you will soon discover what an invaluable tool it is for getting rid of all of those little blips and bits that you couldn't remove with the glasscutter. Bear in mind, though, that when you start to grind a piece of glass, the edge that you are pushing against may still be rough enough to cut you. Once it has been ground, however, you won't cut your fingers when you come to do the foiling and the pieces will also fit together perfectly.

The grinder's grinding wheel is embedded with diamond grit, which is kept wet with a sponge that sits adjacent to it, in a reservoir of water below the top plate. By pushing a piece of glass against this turning wheel and then moving it from side to side, you can obtain a lovely smooth edge.

Many models incorporate a glass safety shield that sits between you and your work, preventing the powdered glass and water from splashing into your eyes, but if your grinder does not have a safety shield, ensure that you wear goggles. It is also vitally important that you keep the water in the reservoir well topped up, as powdered glass is a severe health hazard. Finally, clean out the wet, ground glass in the reservoir at regular intervals to avoid clogging the mechanism.

WIZARD

A glass grinder. The wheel is embedded with diamond grit.

The soldering iron

Soldering irons can either be electric or run off butane gas. An electric one should be a minimum of 75 watts, as the bit has to be large and heavy-duty enough to hold a great deal of heat, otherwise it will grind to a halt halfway down when you are soldering a long 'bead' of solder. It is also advisable to opt for an iron-clad copper bit rather than a simple straight one, because the copper will be eaten away at the tip.

The gas soldering iron has a flame jet which plays on the copper bit which sits at a right angle to the handle. It is a much more expensive option than an electric soldering iron, and is usually only used for large-scale leaded-light work.

Whichever type you choose, ensure that your soldering iron has some kind of stand, as it will become very hot and will scorch anything that it is placed on. When using it, be careful not to touch any part of it except the handle, and do not to let the flex (or anything else) drag across the iron, as the iron will quickly melt the flex down to the bare wires.

Solder

The solder that is nowadays used for copper foilwork is known as 'F grade'. This is a fifty-fifty mix of lead and tin which has a very low melting point, making it flow well. It is perfectly adequate for leaded-light work, although a blow-pipe-grade solder, 40 per cent tin and 60 per cent lead, is often used for this.

Although you can buy solder with a flux core, it should never be used for stained-glass work. This is because although the flux helps the solder to flow, it also prevents it from sticking to the glass when it has been painted on beforehand.

Patina

A patina is a chemical that reacts with the solder to give it a different-coloured finish. Copper sulphate will do this by coating the solder with a thin layer of copper. If other chemicals are added as well, they will leave a dark or antique finish.

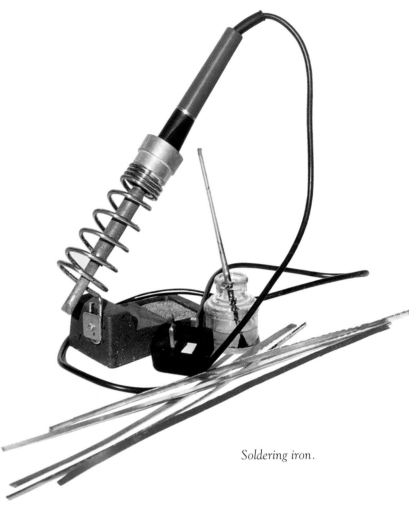

Soldering iron.

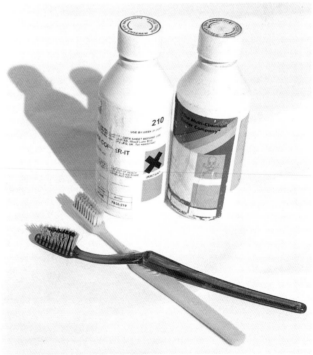

Patina.

Safety first!

It is essential to have a good first-aid kit, which should include such items as plasters, tweezers for removing glass splinters, an eyewash, a spray for treating burns instantly (although ten minutes under a running cold tap will do the same thing) and an antidote gel for hydrofluoric acid.

Rubber gloves are useful for many tasks, and are essential when you are working with acid. A dust mask, or preferably a gas mask suitable for use with acid, should be used if you are etching indoors. Goggles, or protective glasses, and a rubber or PVC apron are also good ideas.

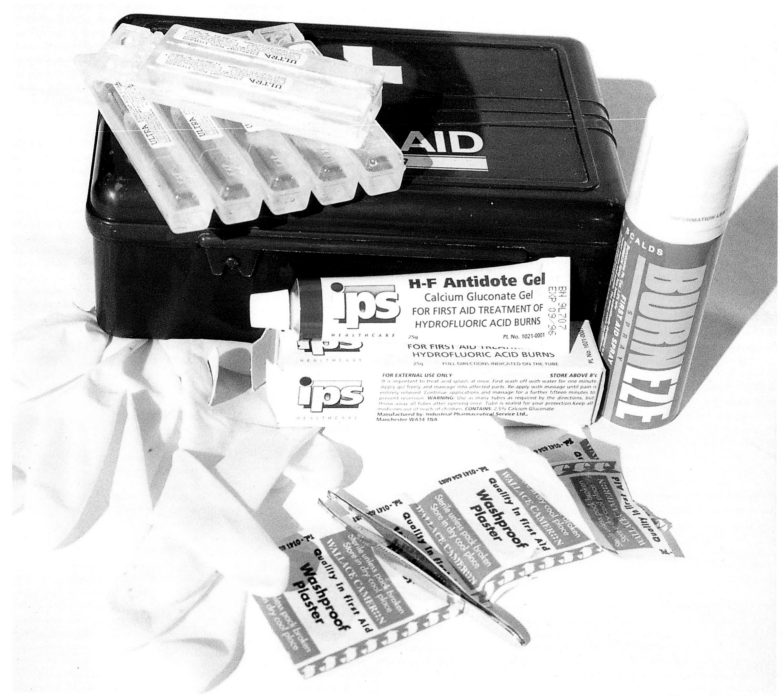

First aid equipment.

CHAPTER 2
Starting out

You'll soon discover that the greater the line of curvature on a piece of glass, the harder it is to cut, and right angles are definitely out. Even if you manage to cut an internal right angle into a piece of glass, it will be structurally unsound and will crack and break when the first vibration hits it. This is one reason to keep your design simple.

In addition, very small pieces of glass are both difficult to foil and are almost certain to be dropped and lost in the pile of the carpet. Working with very long, thin pieces of glass is also not to be recommended as their delicate points will often break off at the cutting stage. Remember, too, that there should be as much contact between the pieces of glass as possible, and that pieces that are joined by just one small point will bend and break away from each other quite quickly.

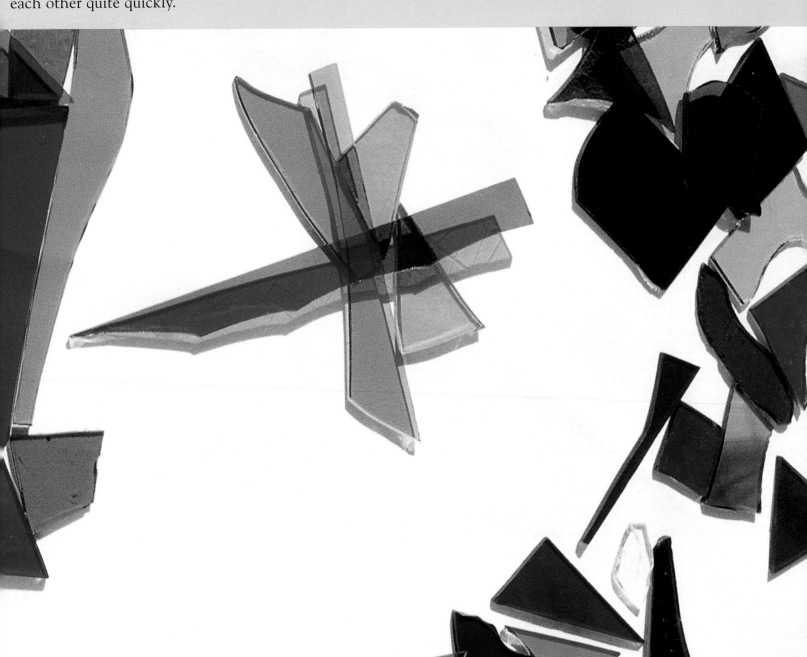

Planning your design

Fig.1.

Fig.2.

Fig.3.

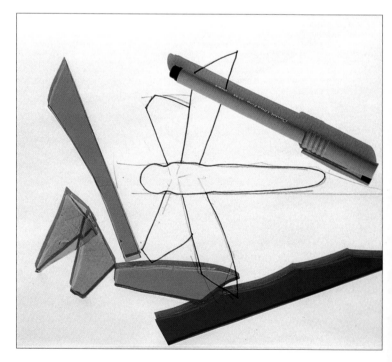

Fig.4.

Look for pictures or photographs of things that you would like to make, for instance, a flower or a fish. Try to simplify the basic shape to as few pieces as possible, rather like making a caricature of a human face. Pick out only the characteristics that give the object its identity and disregard the rest (fig.1).

It is often both easy and fun to create designs from pieces of glass in your cullet box. ('Cullet' is the generic term for small pieces of glass offcuts.) Rather than throwing them away, this is a good way of using up offcuts (fig.2).

Ideas for subjects will often suggest themselves if you play around with different pieces of glass for long enough (fig.3).

I tipped out the contents of my cullet box and sorted through the pieces until the shape of a dragonfly suggested itself (fig.4). Tomorrow it could be a sailing boat, and the day after that a simple flower.

You will probably only need to trim off a bit here and a piece there to create a design that hadn't occurred to you before you started (fig.5). Your design may also take on a life of its own while you are working on it, as in the case of my dragonfly.

Having trimmed the pieces, I decided that the design would be improved by placing the larger wing above the smaller one. It was not too late to change it, so I reground the pieces slightly so that they fitted snugly against both the body and each other (fig.6). You'll probably agree that this was an improvement on the original idea (fig.7).

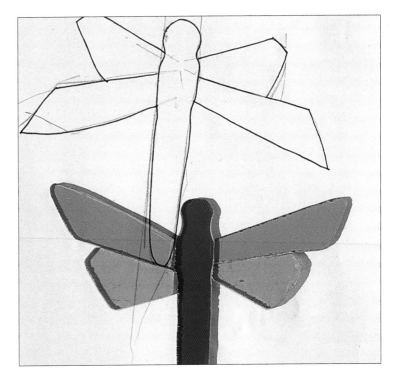

Fig.5.

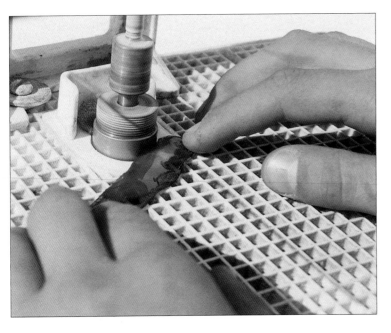

Fig.6.

Fig.7.

How to cut glass

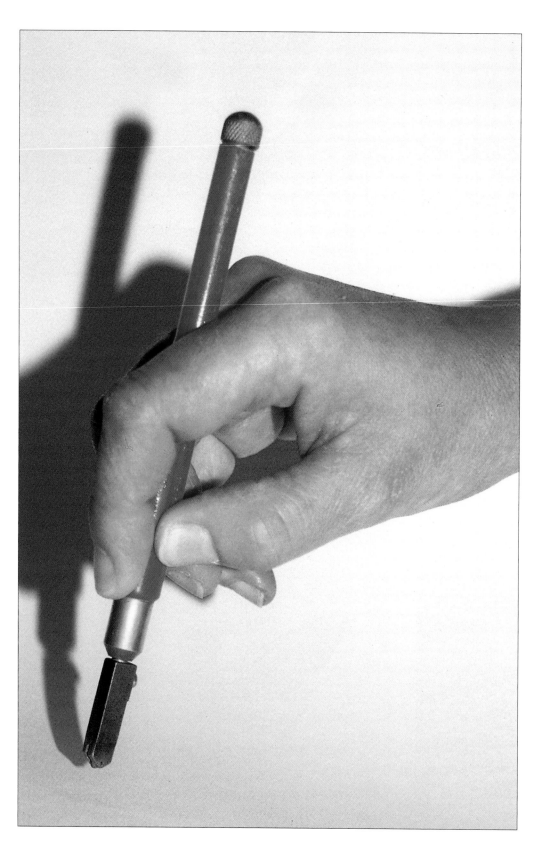

The glasscutter must be held in an upright position and the wheel must be rolled (fig.8). This may sound obvious, but it is amazing how many people try to drag the wheel sideways across the glass, making a sound that sets your teeth on edge (the wheel does not need to be very much out of true to produce this effect).

If you are using a standard-shaped glasscutter rather than a pistol-grip one, you should ideally hold it between your first and second fingers and not between your first finger and thumb, as if you were holding a pencil. This ensures that the glasscutter is kept in an upright position and, being securely held, cannot wobble. If you are using a steel-wheeled cutter that has to be dipped in white spirit, hold it with your index finger resting on the fingerpad at the front. If you are using an oil-filled cutter, make sure that the little screw on the head of the cutter is facing towards you, which is the most comfortable way to hold it.

The little square notches at the back of glasscutters were traditionally used for grozing, or chewing off, bits of glass that did not come off cleanly when the glass was cut. Nowadays we usually use specially designed breaking, or grozing, pliers.

If you are cutting a large sheet of glass against a straight edge for the first time,

Fig.8.

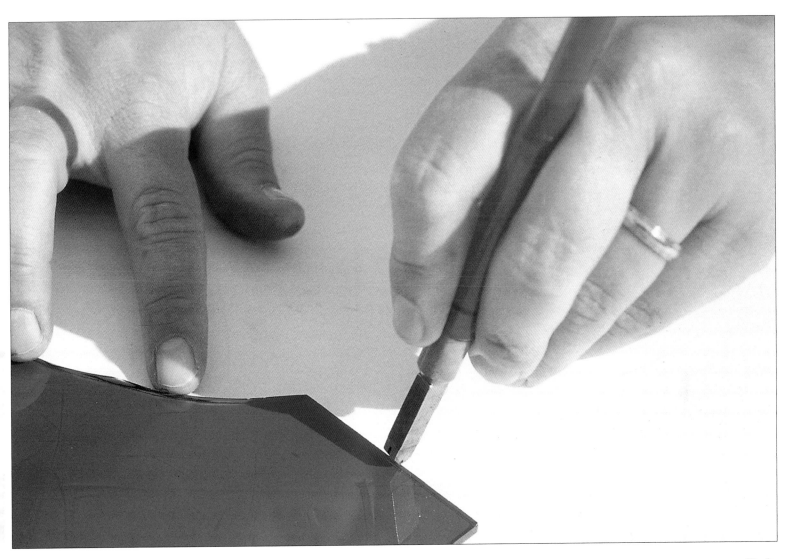

Fig 9.

put the glasscutter at the far side of the sheet and pull it towards you. If you are cutting small pieces of glass to a pattern for a suncatcher, however, it is easier to see the line that you are cutting if you push the glasscutter, which prevents your hand from obscuring the line that you are cutting to. Before moving on to the next stage, I recommend that you practise the following method until you get it right. (It doesn't matter how many score lines you make in an old piece of glass, as your local glass merchant will have boxes full of cullet should you need it.)

Holding the glasscutter securely, place the wheel as close to the near edge of the glass as you can without it slipping off. First push the glasscutter downwards into the glass, so that pressure is applied right from the beginning of the cut, and then push it away from you to the far edge of the glass (fig.9). Do not stop along the way: you must make one continuous line. You should hear a sound as the wheel bites into the surface of the glass and moves all the way across. If you don't hear this sound being made all the way, don't

try to improve the cut line by going over it again, as this will only make matters worse. Remember that what you are trying to do is to break the surface tension of the glass, and that because glass is technically a viscous liquid, it is less likely to break in the right place if you make more than one score line. Going over the same line again will also considerably reduce your glasscutter's life expectancy.

If you find that you produce no sound at all when you are pushing the glasscutter across the glass, you may need to use your other hand to push down on the top of the glasscutter to put more pressure on it. Although successful glasscutting has more to do with having the knack rather than applying brute force, it is often helpful to start with brute force and then to work towards developing that knack at a later stage. To cut a curved line, use the same procedure as you would for scoring a straight line.

When you have made a score line that sounds as if it has taken all

the way across the glass, put down your glasscutter and, with your knuckles and thumbs together, parallel to each side of the cut, grip the glass at the near edge (fig.10). The glass should be facing away from you, so that any chips do not fly into your face. Now roll your knuckles apart to break the glass (fig.11). The technique and amount of force needed are similar to those used when breaking a piece of chocolate off a bar. Many people do not feel confident about doing this, but if you keep your hands together as you carry out the manoeuvre, it should not be possible to be cut by the glass. If, however, your hands are apart, the glass may slip and cut you across the back of the knuckles.

After the score has been made, it is sometimes necessary to tap it underneath the glass to start the breaking process especially on a curved score line. Do this with the other end of the glasscutter, which has a metal knob on it, and hold it in the same position as you would for cutting, but upside down (fig.12). Aim to use a pincer movement, like a crab's, holding your thumb on top of the glass while you tap the score line from underneath with the knob. The advantage of tapping the cut like this is that if the glass suddenly breaks you will be holding the piece that comes off, rather than it falling on the work surface and possibly breaking.

Fig 10.

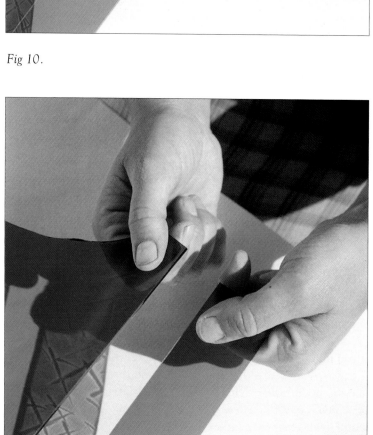

Fig 11.

Fig 12.

Fig 13.

If you find it difficult to hit the glass sharply enough to crack it in this way, an easier method is to turn the scored glass upside down, placing it on enough layers of newspaper to provide a yielding surface, and then to tap it gently (fig.13). Much less force is required to crack the glass in this way, so err on the side of caution and tap gently more than once in order to avoid ending up with a pile of fragments. Don't forget to turn the glass around again, so that the score line is on the upper side, before trying to break it. Once you have tapped the cut and started the break successfully, it is then possible to hold it with your hands, as for the straight-line cut, and then to bend it apart. You will see the glass tearing along the line until it breaks in two.

Alternatively, if it is a very small piece of glass, or you are nervous about breaking it, you could use breaking pliers. Place the edge of the pliers parallel to the cut line and then bend the glass apart (fig.14). Remember that glass that has been cut on the curve often has a nasty under-cut edge and can therefore be much more dangerous to handle than a straight-edged piece.

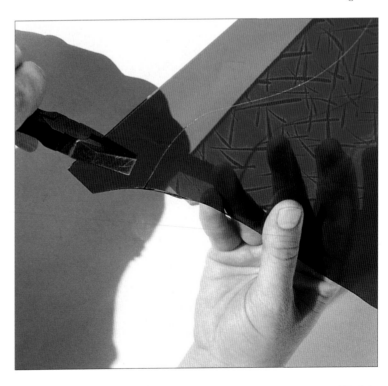

Fig 14.

Fig 15.

It is advisable to remove this under-cut edge immediately, before you cut yourself, using either the grinder, wet carborundum stone or another piece of glass scraped along the edge (fig.15). To cut some of the larger straight-sided pieces for the terrarium and lampshade, you will need to use a straight edge (this technique is covered in the mosaic mirror project (see page 65).

For some of the projects in this book, you will need to use a bottle with the top cut off. Although you can buy a bottlecutter, this will only cut a straight line around a round bottle. If you want to cut an irregularly-shaped bottle or an undulating line – which is more interesting – you can only do this with a handheld glasscutter.

Using a pen, first mark the line on the bottle (fig.16). Then, placing your fingers against the bottle to stop the glasscutter skidding, score a line around the bottle along the pen line, making sure that the end of your line meets the original point (fig.17).

Fig 16.

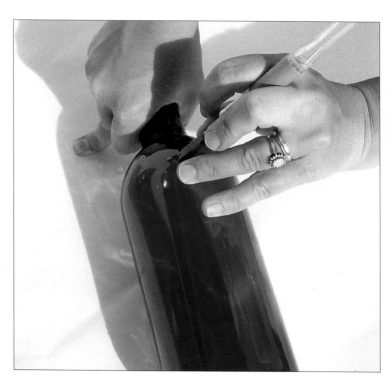

Fig 17.

Holding the bottle over a plastic bowl or sink, pour boiling water over the cut, taking care not to scald your fingers (fig.18). When it has been thoroughly heated, run the cut under a cold tap immediately. If the tap runs too slowly, the cut won't break, while if it runs too fast, the cut will crack right around and sometimes down the bottle, too. Only by trial and error will you discover the exact speed of flow needed.

When you get it right, the bottle will crack all the way round and you can then lift off the top, which will make a slight popping sound, leaving a clean edge (fig.19). This now only needs to be neatened with the grinder or be given a light dusting with a wet carborundum stone (fig.20).

Because it is embedded with diamond grit, the wheel on the grinder is very expensive, so the more accurately you cut your glass on your first attempt, the less often you will have to use the grinder and the longer the wheel will last. The wheel is, however, very useful for removing sharp edges and grinding pieces to fit exactly where required. After the pieces of glass have been ground, and before they are foiled, they must be washed in boiling water, which, contrary to popular belief, will not crack the glass. While they are still hot, carefully remove them from the water, place them on some newspaper and dry them with a paper towel. This will remove any fingermarks, residual powdered glass and white spirit left by the glasscutter, rendering the pieces of glass grease-free and ready for foiling.

Fig 18.

Fig 19.

Fig 20.

Foiling

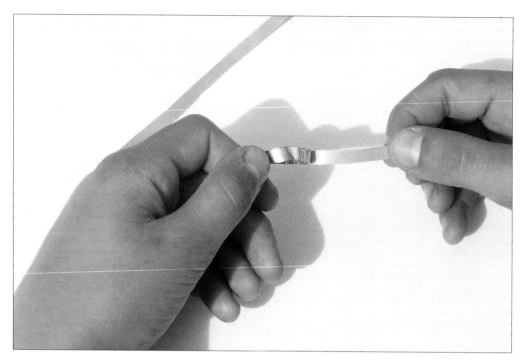

Fig 21.

To thread the handfoiler, take a reel of copper foil, separate the foil from its backing paper to a length of about 2.5 centimetres (1 inch) and then curl the backing paper downwards, away from the foil, using your thumbnail (fig.21).

If you look at a spare length of backing paper, you will notice that the side that lay against the adhesive is shiny and that the other side has a matt finish. If you take the matt side, the copper foil will adhere to it, making a little 'leader' that will not stick to the handfoiler as you thread it (fig.22). It is almost impossible, and very frustrating, to try to thread the foil without this leader attached, as the foil will stick to everything it touches.

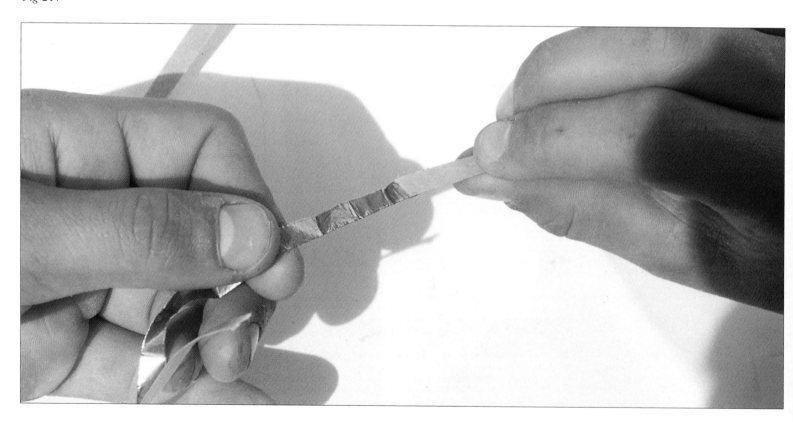

Fig 22.

Thread both the backing paper and the foil – with its leader – through the tiny slot at the back of the handfoiler, with the copper side uppermost (fig.23).

As the backing paper goes through the slot, it should almost immediately emerge from another slot underneath the foiler. The copper foil itself, however, along with its leader, should continue up the shaft of the foiler, (fig.25) coming out at the top end beneath a little roller .

Pull the leader through and cut it off. Your handfoiler has now been threaded (fig.26).

When holding the foiler, be careful not to touch the foil as it travels up the shaft of the tool, as it will then adhere to the foiler and won't emerge from the top. Pull about 60 to 90 centimetres

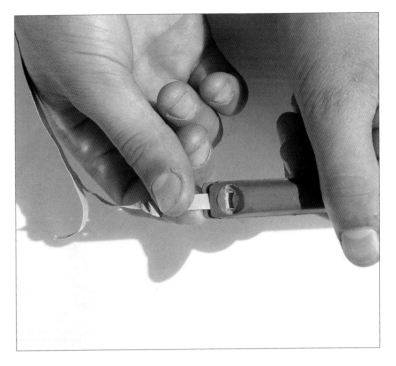

Fig 23.

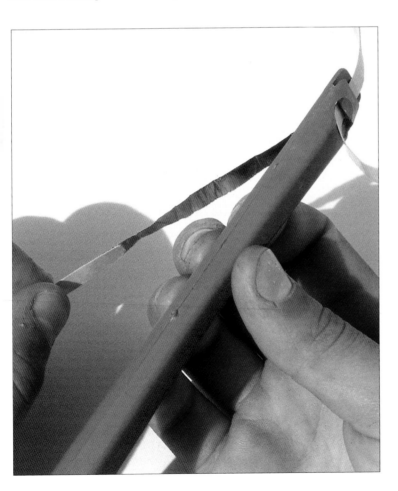

Fig 24.

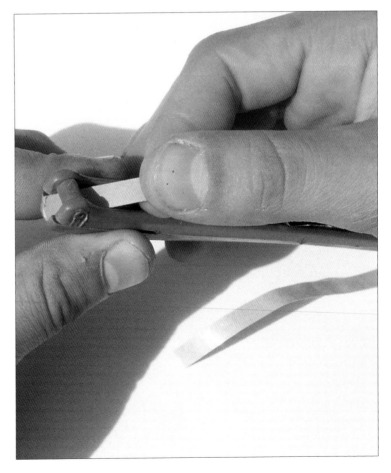

Fig 25.

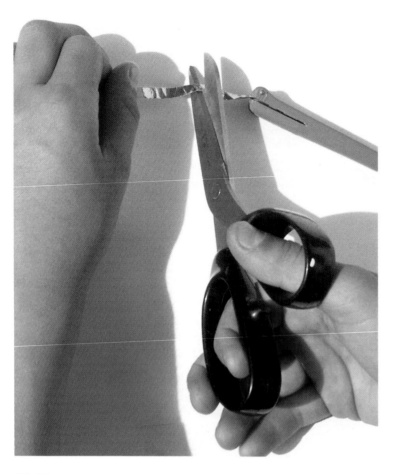

Fig 26.

(2 or 3 feet) of slack from the roll before starting work. If there is not sufficient slack, the foil is likely to twist and snag before entering the foiler, thus jamming it.

If you take the foiler in your hand and turn it upside down, so that the adhesive side of the foil is facing you, you will notice a channel in the back of the foiler, which is about the same width as the thickness of your glass. Take the piece of glass to be foiled and place it in this channel, which is designed to centre the foil on the edge of the glass, with an equal amount of overlap on each side. As you pull the glass through the channel, the little roller at the top of the foiler will then push the copper foil onto the edge (fig.27). (It usually works much better if the foiler is held still and the piece of glass is moved round rather than the other way around.)

Although the foiler is designed to remove the backing paper from the foil, it often doesn't, and if the paper rides up inside the handle of the tool, it may be necessary to keep pulling it back down, otherwise the foil will emerge from under the roller with the backing paper still attached, which means that it can't adhere to the glass.

When you have gone right round the glass and have returned to your starting point, overlap the first bit of copper foil by about 1.25 centimetres (½ inch) and then break or cut the foil (fig.28). Using your finger and thumb, crimp the free edges of the foil over the edges of the glass.

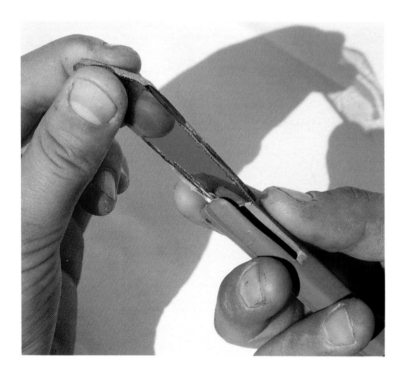

Fig 27.

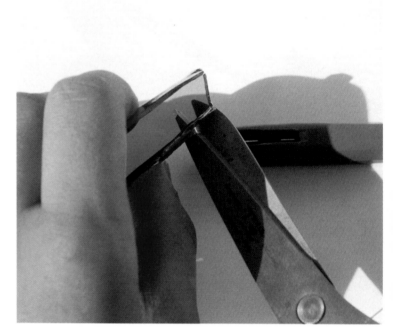

Fig 28.

Fig 29.

Always push slightly inwards, towards the middle of the piece of glass, as it is quite easy to cut yourself on the foil if you're not careful. On corners, first tuck in one side and then overlap it with the adjacent side to leave a neat finish (fig.29).

Using a fid, go round the edge of each piece of glass, flattening the copper foil on both sides and ensuring that it has adhered securely to the glass so that the flux will not seep out later (fig.30). If a crackling sound seems to coming from the foil as you use the fid, it indicates that it has not stuck properly and must be peeled off, washed and dried thoroughly and then replaced to prevent your work from falling apart later on.

Once you have foiled all of the pieces for your item, place them on a board ready for soldering.

Fig 30.

Soldering

Fig 31.

Fig 32.

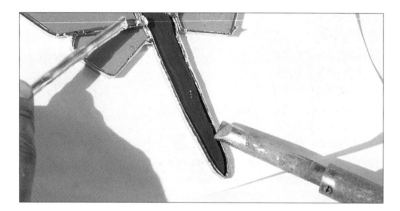

Fig 33.

Fig 34.

Your work must now be fluxed before it can be soldered. You will find a little – preferably spill-proof – jar for the flux useful, as well as an old, small paintbrush. Pour a little safety flux into the jar and then, using the brush, flux generously over all of the copper foil, also going a little way onto the glass (fig.31). Not only will this make the solder adhere to the copper foil securely, but it will also ensure that the solder does not stick to the glass, instead rolling off it. Because many people forget to flux their work on the second side if they leave it till later, it is probably best to flux both sides at this stage.

Place all of the pieces of glass for your suncatcher in their correct positions and then carefully drop a little bead of solder onto as many points on your work as is necessary to hold it together (fig.32). Try not to touch the work with the soldering iron, because the slightest movement may knock the pieces out of position while the solder is setting. Once the cardinal points have been attached, your pieces will be held together to form a unified item.

You now have to 'tin' the perimeter of your work, that is, apply a thin coating of solder to it. Wipe the hot soldering-iron bit across the end of the stick of solder and stroke it down the work's foiled edge (fig.33).

Once you have coated the perimeter foil, you then have to build up the piece's internal joints with thicker beads of solder – a good exercise in hand-eye co-ordination.

Tipping the soldering iron on its edge, so that only the corner of the bit touches the work and the flat face is facing towards you, try to melt just sufficient solder onto this plate and then trickle it off the bottom point onto your joint, keeping the edge of the bit in contact with the foil (fig.34). Try to maintain a consistent speed and to form a raised bead of solder that is not so flat that you can see the form of the foil beneath it, but not so thick that it is lumpy and uneven. The glass should not crack, firstly because the copper foil, which is a good conductor, will dissipate the heat very quickly, and, secondly, because since you are soldering on the edge of the glass, it has room to expand. (If you were to touch the middle of a piece of glass with a hot soldering iron for any length of time, it would probably crack

You will only run a neat bead of solder after a great deal of practice, so don't become discouraged at this stage if you're not satisfied with the neatness of your bead (and you almost certainly won't be at first). Don't try prodding or dabbing it with a hot soldering iron. This will only make matters worse, as you will melt a small area of the solder, which, as you pull the iron away, will form a peak and set as a sharp point. If you want to re-do it, flux the bead again and run the iron down the whole length of it without using any more solder (there will almost certainly be sufficient on the joint already).

A reasonable length of the bead should be melted at any one time as you are working on it, enabling the solder to find its own level in its liquid state before setting to ensure a smooth, even bead. If you move the iron too fast, the bead will melt on the top surface only, leaving leave a rough, uneven line of solder with dragmarks in it. If you move the iron too slowly, on the other hand, especially on a three-dimensional piece of work, the solder will disappear down the little crack in the middle, never to be seen again. Only time, patience and practice will help you to overcome these problems. Don't worry at this stage about any excess solder on the outer edge of the work: this will be melted in at a later stage.

Once you have soldered all of the joints on one side of your work, turn it over. Ensure that all of the copper has been well fluxed on

the reverse side and then repeat the tinning process around the edge, also building up the beads on the internal joints.

You now need to finish the outer edge of the work. It is advisable to pick up the work with a paper towel at this stage, as it will have become fairly hot. Keeping your hand well covered with the paper towel, hold your suncatcher vertically to flux the outside edge. (The paper towel should prevent your hand from being scalded if any solder drips or splashes onto it.) If your suncatcher has any straight edges, start with these, as they are easier to work on than curved edges. There may either be enough solder on the outer edge already, in which case it only needs to be redistributed, or you may need to add a little more. The solder on the outer edge should be as thick as you can make it without it actually dripping off. You should not be able to see the square edges of the glass under the foil. Because the foil is very thin, the more solder you can add to it, the stronger the edge will become.

Melt the solder along this edge with the corner, not the flat, of the bit (fig.35). This will lay the solder onto the work rather than scraping it off. The edge that you are soldering must be kept completely horizontal to the workbench, because, in its molten state, the solder will run with gravity, and any tilt from the horizontal will cause it to run off the foil. This is hard enough to do on a straight edge, but when you have a curve – either convex or concave – it is ten times more so. If you don't think that you already have enough solder on the edge, it is often helpful to place little buttons of solder along it, which will as reservoirs that you can pick up with the iron as you pass.

Fig 35.

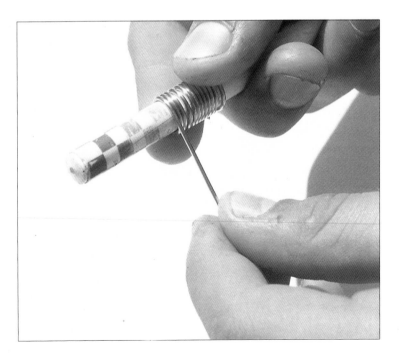

Fig 36.

Fig 37.

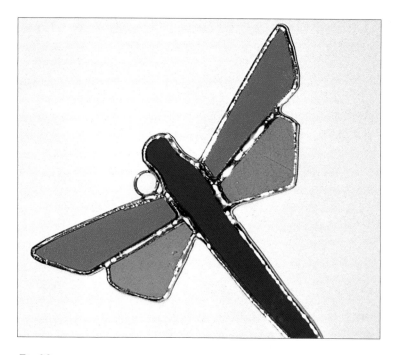

Fig 38.

Flux the curved edge and melt the solder along it using one smooth, continuous movement. It is much easier to hold the soldering iron still and to move the suncatcher slowly, rather than the other way round, making sure that the part that you are soldering is kept horizontal at all times. This will ensure that solder will have set before you turn the work to an angle at which it would otherwise drip. (If you get it wrong, you will realise why covering your hand with a paper towel was a good idea.)

When soldering, you may sometimes find that there is a bit of solder which, no matter what you do, refuses to lie flat when the soldering iron leaves it. In such cases, dab a little flux onto the solder (which, true to the Latin origins of the word, will make the solder 'flow'), reapply the iron, and you should then find that it behaves itself perfectly. Another problem that you may encounter is melting the stick of solder onto your piece in error, where it then sets before you can remove it, leaving your prized artwork looking like a lollipop. If this happens to you, don't panic and pull at it, which, along with the solder, would remove the copper foil. Because it got there by being melted, melt it again by touching your soldering iron against it, and you should then find that it comes away easily.

To hang your work, you will need a small copper ring, which you can easily make by stripping the outer sheath from some electrical flex with a sharp craft knife to reveal the copper wire underneath. (You will find the flex easier to strip if you place it in a washing-up bowl and pour boiling water over it.) A length of copper wire can then be wound around a pencil or biro and the rings clipped off one at a time as you need them (fig.36). For the suncatcher, take one of these copper rings, and, holding it with a small pair of long-nosed pliers, first flux the two open ends of the ring and then melt a small bead of solder onto them to join them (fig 37).

Find the suncatcher's balance point by carefully holding it up between your finger and thumb until it hangs straight (remember that the flux is oily and your work may drop or break). Where your finger and thumb meet is the balance point to which you should attach the ring. (It is now advisable to abut your work against something immovable, otherwise you may end up chasing it around the board.) Apply some more flux to the balance point, as well as to the ring, and then, holding the ring firmly with the pliers, place it against the edge of the suncatcher and touch it with the hot soldering iron until it fuses to the edge.

Gently wash off the flux with a little washing-up liquid mixed with plenty of hot water and then dry the suncatcher with paper towels. It can now be hung in a sunny window, where it will catch the light and throw colours around the room (fig.38). The solder will eventually become dull, but if you prefer it to remain shiny, you can polish it with a metal-cleaning preparation. If, on the other hand, you prefer the solder coppered or darkened, paint it with the appropriate patina, which will react with the solder and coat it with a copper or black finish.

CHAPTER 3
Glass painting

Vase or night-light holder

This is a very simple technique, which anyone who has done marbling on paper will recognise, using the principle that spirit floats on water and does not mix with it. Different shapes and sizes of receptacles will suggest different uses. A tall, narrow bottle, for example, would make an unusual candleholder, while if you cut it below the neck, you have a handy-sized vase. You could also dip a mixing basin to make an attractive fruit bowl or perhaps provide a container for a display of floating candles.

Equipment and materials
clean 4 litre (1 gallon) ice-cream box
or similar
2 or 3 different-coloured, spirit-based
glass paints
clear jam jar or bottle with the top
cut off (see page 26)
newspaper
white spirit
paper towels

1. Fill the ice cream box about three-quarters full of cold water. (Bear in mind that the jar or bottle will be dipped in the water and will therefore will displace some of it, so it is advisable to test how much water will be displaced before adding the glass paint). Add a small amount of one or two colours (and a maximum of three) of glass paint, pouring it gently onto the surface of the water.

2. Gently move the coloured paints around so that they create a marbled effect on the surface of the water.

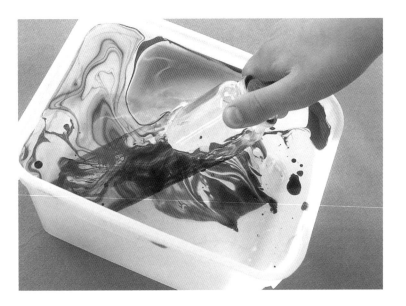

3. Make sure that the jam jar or bottle is dry, and then dip it slowly into the water up to its neck, but not so far that water enters the jar.

4. Lift out the jar or bottle. As you remove it from the water, your first layer of paint will be coated with a second, producing interesting patterns of overlapping colours. You will probably find that bold swirls of colour work better than overmixed ones.

5. Place the jar or bottle on some clean, dry newspaper and allow it to dry naturally for at least 24 hours. Do not touch the paint while it is drying, to avoid dislodging or smudging it.

6. Depending on the height and size of the vessel that you dipped, you can use it either as a vase or a night-light holder. In a later chapter we will be dealing with acid-etching glass (see page 54), which gives it an opaque finish. If the glass-painting technique is used on an acid-etched jar, it will give out a glow without the candle being visible.

Painted roundel

A roundel is a circle of glass that has a protective edge of lead. Any simple design can be painted onto it to brighten up a window that doesn't look out over much of a view. I have given you a choice of a seahorse or a poppy design to get you started. A painted glass roundel is intended to look like real stained glass, with thick, black lines around it. Don't be tempted to try to make it look like watercolour painting. Go for the bold, rather than subtle, approach. Most makes of glass paint do not include a white because white is simply an absence of colour, so if you want an element of your design to appear white, don't paint it. The darker the colour you paint around it, the lighter this area will seem.

Equipment and Materials
template p122
pencil
paper
1 plain-glass roundel (obtainable from good craft stores), 10 centimetres (4 inches) or 17.5 centimetres (7 inches) in diameter
paper towels for cleaning
methylated spirits
outline relief paste in the colour of your choice
sharp craft knife
3 or 4 different-coloured glass paints
paintbrushes
white spirit, cellulose thinner or water for cleaning, depending on the base of your glass paint

1. If you are working to your own design, firstly place the roundel on a piece of paper and draw around it with a pencil. Next, draw an inner circle, so that you have allowed for the width of the lead around the edge. Keep the design fairly simple, as the outline relief will leave quite a thick line. Remember that the raised relief acts as a barrier between colours, so each area must be completely contained by the outline, otherwise colours will flow into each other and may blur the design. Clean the glass roundel thoroughly, using some paper towels and methylated spirits.

2. Place the roundel on your design and, using the outline relief, carefully trace the design onto the glass. The neatest way to do this is to squeeze a tiny amount of the relief paste from the tube's long nozzle and then to lift it away from the glass a little, so that it lays the paste on the glass from above. This technique is rather like icing a cake, and will leave a much smoother line than if the nozzle is in contact with the glass. When you near the end of the line that you are tracing, stop putting pressure on the tube and lower the last residue onto the glass, so that the nozzle touches the surface of the glass again as you reach the end of the line.

3. Now set the roundel aside in a warm, dry place where it will not be disturbed, as the outline relief is liable to smudge for some time after it has been applied. When the outline relief is completely dry, neaten up any mistakes. Using a sharp craft knife, carefully trim away any blobs or over-runs and then peel them off, taking care not to dislodge the parts that you want to keep.

4. Depending on the type of your design, begin painting either in the middle and then work outwards, or at the top, working down to the bottom. Either way, you are less likely to smudge the areas that you have already painted as you are working. If you have used outline relief, the glass paint can be laid on fairly thickly, as it will not go beyond the barrier.

5. It is also possible, as I have done, to lay the paint on using a medicine dropper, which should leave a more even finish because the paint will find its own level. If you have used a black pen, however, you will not be able to lay the paint on so thickly, as it will run over the black line into the next colour. Although you may find that your brush strokes are visible, if you use them creatively, you can make them work to your advantage. If you are painting sea, for instance, you can make the brush strokes look like little waves. If you are painting a dolphin, you can start the brush stroke at its nose, and sweep down to its tail.

When you have finished, leave the roundel to dry flat, preferably in a dust-free environment, as any particles that are in the air will soon settle on the paint and will cement themselves irrevocably to it. It is safest to leave the roundel for 24 hours before hanging it, especially if the glass paint is particularly thick.

In the case of young children, or people whose hands are not very steady, it may be easier to use a black poster pen, which creates an opaque line. Because it isn't raised, it will not act as a barrier, however, and you will have to be slightly more careful when applying the glass paints. While the pen line takes only take a minute or so to dry, the outline relief requires a couple of hours to be on the safe side

Greetings cards

Equipment and Materials
template p121
A4-sized sheet of transparent acetate
(the type used for overhead
projectors is ideal)
cutting board
sharp craft knife
outline relief
coloured glass paints of your choice
A4-sized white card
sharp pencil
double-sided sticky tape or photo
mounts
silver or gold pen

Although this is technically not a stained-glass project, more of a stained-acetate one, because it uses glass paints, it makes an interesting and simple project. Once you have mastered the technique, you will think of many occasions on which a card could be sent that had never occurred to you before. The cards will be treasured by their recipients, too, who may tape them to a window.

1. Take the sheet of acetate, and cut it into six by firstly bisecting it lengthways and then cutting each of these sections into three equal pieces. Place a piece of film over one of the templates in this book (you may find it helpful to tack it gently into position so that it does not move). Trace the outline with the outline relief and leave it to dry.

2. Using several different colours, fill each area of the design with glass paint and leave them to dry.

3. Fold the white card in half, with the shorter sides together. Then fold the card in half the other way, to form a standing card shape. (All of the designs that I have given you are suitable for a vertical format, but you could also design your own card for a horizontal format.) Cut a narrow piece of acetate to leave room for your message below, and remember that if you want a side-opening card in this format, the first fold of the card must be made with the long sides together.

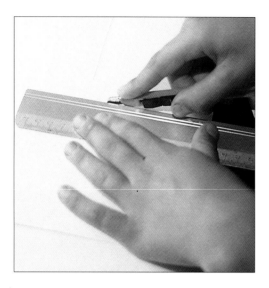

4. Cut a template the same size as your design and place it just above the centre on the front of the card, thereby leaving a larger margin at the bottom for your message. Draw around this square. Unfold the card, place it on the cutting board and, using the craft knife, cut out the square.

5. Refold the card and, using a sharp pencil, mark the corners on the lower sheet, so that you will know where to position your acetate.

6. Neatly write your message ('Happy birthday', 'Congratulations' or whatever is relevant to the occasion). It is easier to position the message centrally when the card is folded. If it ends up being a little off-centre, however, fill the space with a small motif – a star, for instance.

7. Unfold the card again. Using the pencilled corners drawn earlier as a guide, stick down your design with either double-sided sticky tape or photo mounts.

8. I have given you enough designs to cover nearly every eventuality, but I am sure that you can come up with plenty of your own. Remember to keep them uncomplicated and bold, which is not only simpler, but also has greater impact.

Painted glass bowl

Equipment and Materials
template p119
white paper
pencil
1 medium-sized Pyrex mixing bowl or
the bottom half of a pickled-onion
jar or similar (see page 26)
masking tape (optional)
ice-cream box filled with screwed-up
newspaper
methylated spirits
cleaning cloth
outline relief
4 or 5 different-coloured glass paints
water
white spirit or cellulose thinner for
cleaning, depending on the glass-
paint base
paintbrushes

Applying outline relief and glass paint to a curved surface is much more difficult than applying them to a flat one, as gravity plays a part. As you work around the bowl, it also becomes much easier accidentally to smudge the far side of the work. It is therefore best to complete one section at a time. Patience is essential for this project, and the saying 'More haste, less speed' is certainly true in this case. If you smudge either the outline relief or the paint, there is little alternative but to wipe it off and start all over again.

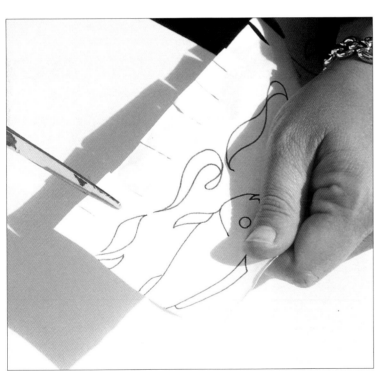

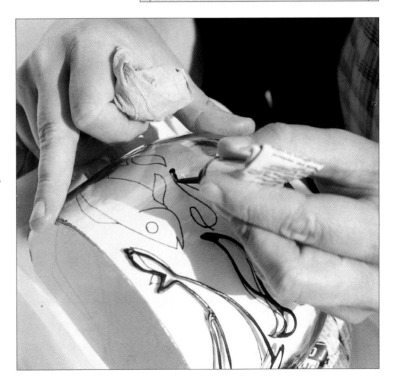

1. Cut a strip of white paper whose width is equal to the depth of the bowl and whose length equals the circumference of the inside of the bowl. Draw your design onto the paper, making sure that the ends of your design meet up to form a continuous frieze. It may help to tape your design to the inside of the bowl so that it doesn't move while you are tracing it with the outline relief.

2. Place the bowl in the newspaper-filled ice-cream box, which will act as a support, and hold the bowl on its side. Using the outline relief, start tracing your design onto the glass, holding the nozzle fractionally above the glass as you work. To avoid smudging your work as you go round, when you have traced approximately a quarter of your design, leave it to dry before continuing with the next section.

45

3. Now you can begin to use the glass paints. Remember that you should paint only a section at a time, otherwise gravity will cause the paints to leak over the outline-relief barrier and to run into the next section. The paint must at least be tacky before you move the bowl around to start the next section.

4. You will need to curb your impatience in order not to ruin your work. The wait will be worth it, however, as you will end up with a beautiful bowl that you could fill with potpourri or sea shells to grace any bathroom.

CHAPTER 4
Glass etching

Named mirror tile

Equipment and Materials
template p118
sheet of sticky-back plastic
1 15.25, 23 or 30.5 centimetre (6, 9
or 12 inch)
square mirror tile
small, sharp craft knife or scalpel
soft cloth
soft and sharp pencils
computer print-out of the designated
name and small motif(s)
sticky tape
white spirit
newspaper
rubber gloves
etching paste
chunky, hogs-hair paintbrush and
plastic container to hold it
lots of fresh water
old washing-up bowl and brush
bicarbonate of soda
paper towels

Because etching paste contains hydrofluoric acid, which is a very dangerous substance, the etching stage of this process must be carried out in a well-ventilated area, preferably outside, or using a fume-extractor fan. I have chosen to create my design on a 23 centimetre (9 inch) mirror tile, which you can buy in packs, from do-it-yourself stores.

A computer is very useful for creating the lettering for the mirror. Type the name of the person to whom you wish to give the mirror and select a font that is simple, bold and will be easy to cut (remember that you have to do this freehand, using a small craft knife). It's also nice to incorporate a small motif. I have included two that you can use or, alternatively, you could design your own. Remember, though, to keep it simple.

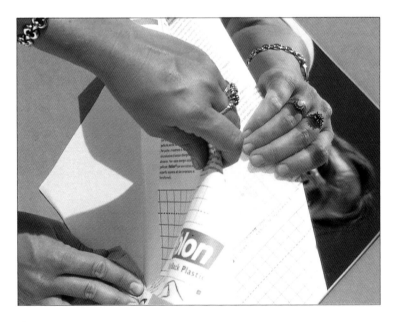

1. You will need to cover the mirror with sticky-backed plastic, which the acid won't react with. Using a sharp craft knife, cut a piece of plastic approximately 1.25 centimetres (½ inch) larger all round than your tile. Peel back one corner of the plastic and stick it to the mirror so that it overlaps the edge.

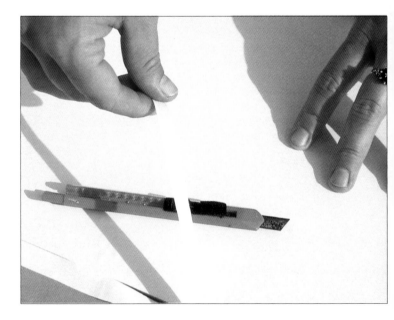

2. Carefully peel off the rest of the backing paper, rubbing it down with a soft cloth held in your other hand as you work from corner to corner to smooth out any bubbles that may have become trapped between the plastic and the surface of the mirror. Carefully trim back the plastic to the edge of the glass.

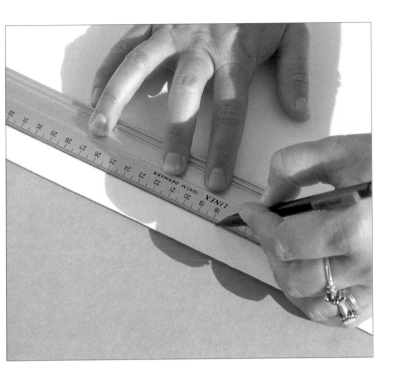

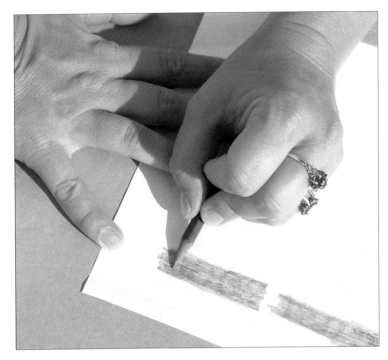

3. Draw a horizontal pencil line approximately 2.5 centimetres (1 inch) above the bottom of the mirror. This is the line that your lettering will sit on. If you have chosen a font whose letters have very long tails, however, you may need to draw the line slightly further away from the edge of the mirror.

4. Turn the computer print-out upside down and rub over the back of it with a soft pencil until it has become completely blackened. Turn the print-out around again and, using sticky tape, stick it to the plastic covering, ensuring that the lettering sits on the pencil line and is parallel with the edge of the mirror.

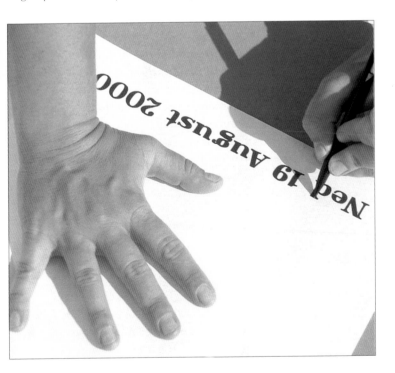

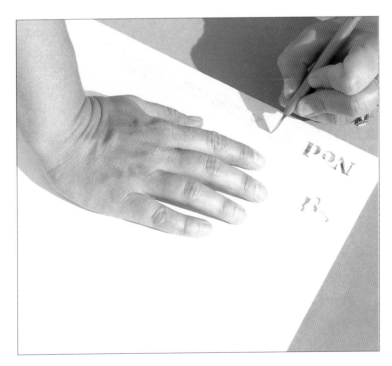

5. Using a sharp pencil, carefully trace the outlines of the letters, which should appear as marks on the plastic. Do the same with the motif, positioning it just beyond the point at which the lettering stops, or at the top corner if there is insufficient room.

6. Using a sharp craft knife or scalpel, cut this line through the plastic and carefully peel off the letters and motif. Small patches of adhesive may be left on the surface of the glass, which you should carefully clean off with a little white spirit and a soft cloth.

7. Place the mirror on some newspaper in a well-ventilated place, put on the rubber gloves, remove the lid from the jar of etching paste, and, using the hogs-hair paintbrush, carefully lay the paste onto the exposed areas of mirror fairly thickly. Replace lid on the jar immediately. Once all of the exposed areas have been covered, keep the paste moving by swirling it around gently with the brush to avoid the etched texture becoming patchy. This should be done at regular intervals over the next 10 to 15 minutes, by which time the paste should have etched the mirror sufficiently.

8. Using a washing-up brush, wash the etching paste off the mirror in a washing-up bowl filled with lots of fresh water, nullify any residual acidity with bicarbonate of soda and then discard the water – preferably down an outside drain. Once you have removed all traces of the etching paste, check the edges and back of your mirror to ensure that none remains. It is now safe to remove your rubber gloves.

Carefully peel off the sticky-back plastic, and, using a soft cloth and some white spirit, polish the mirror tile to remove any residual adhesive. These tiles usually come with a set of sticky pads to fix them to walls (the only surface to which they will not adhere is a washable wallpaper) Mirrors etched with names and dates make ideal presents with an individual touch for christenings, weddings or birthdays.

Ned 19 August 2000

House name

This rather subtle-looking technique will add a touch of distinction to the most humble dwelling. If your house doesn't have a name, enlarge the numbers given in the previous project and use them instead. You could even include your family name. I have designed an ivy motif to decorate the edge, but if you prefer to create your own design, so much the better.

Equipment and Materials
sheet of sticky-back plastic
20.3 x 30.5 centimetre x 3 millimetre
(8 x 12 x ⅛ inch) clear glass
small, sharp craft knife or scalpel
soft cloth
soft and sharp pencils
computer print-out of the designated
name or number and small motif(s)
sticky tape
white spirit
newspaper
rubber gloves
etching paste
chunky, hogs-hair paintbrush and
plastic container to hold it
lots of fresh water
old washing-up bowl and brush
bicarbonate of soda
wooden frame for the glass

1. Cut and apply the sticky-backed plastic to the clear glass as described on page 45, ensuring that there are no bubbles between the plastic and glass.

2. Transfer the name or number of your house, as well as your chosen motif and cut out the characters with a sharp craft knife.

3. (right) Carry out the etching process exactly as before (see page 50), remembering to wear rubber gloves. When washing off the etching paste, be careful not to let any acid-contaminated water come into contact with the back of the glass, as this will cause a slight milkiness if it is left for any length of time (even when it is very diluted, the acid will still etch glass).

4. (below) Once you have removed the sticky-back plastic and have cleaned the piece of glass, mount it in a wooden frame and hang in a window next to your front door.

If this project has left you feeling adventurous, you may be able to replace an existing glass door panel using this technique. Remember, however, that glass for doors must be toughened. Measure the size of the panel right into the rebate and then deduct 3 millimetres ($\frac{1}{8}$ inch) from the horizontal and vertical measurements, which should give you the correct size of glass required. If you ask a professional glazier to cut the glass to size for you, it will be sent away to be toughened by heat treatment. The acid will not eat sufficiently deeply into the top surface of the toughened glass to weaken it, making this method of decoration perfectly safe. The etching process must, of course, be carried out before the glass is inserted into the aperture.

Decorated glass jar

Acid-etching texture on glass will partially obscure anything behind it, making it an ideal way of hiding flower stems in a vase. Your artwork will also be displayed better against a dark background, such as foliage. If you stand your vase in strong sunlight when it is empty, the etch will appear very white and the little boats will seem to be racing each other.

Equipment and Materials
template p125
sheet of sticky-back plastic
a jar or bottle that has been cut in half
small, sharp craft knife or scalpel
soft cloth
Blu-tack (optional)
straight edge
soft and sharp pencils
a template of the design (optional)
sticky tape
white spirit
newspaper
rubber gloves
etching paste
chunky, hogs-hair paintbrush and plastic container to hold it
old washing-up bowl and brush
lots of fresh water
bicarbonate of soda

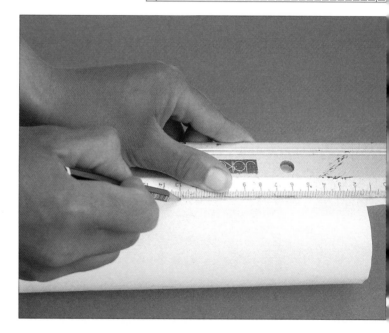

1. Cut a piece of sticky-backed plastic high enough to cover the jar or bottle and long enough to surround it with an overlap of about 1.25 centimetres (½ inch). Peel back a corner of the backing paper and stick to the jar or bottle, carefully peeling off the rest as you smooth the plastic over the jar or bottle until you have covered it and the plastic overlaps.

2. Place the jar or bottle on its side and secure it in some way (ideally with Blu-tack) to prevent it from rolling. Using a straightedge, draw a vertical straight line down the length of the jar or bottle, roughly in the middle of the overlapped section of plastic.

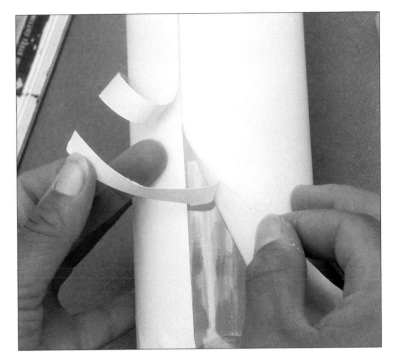

3. Using a sharp knife, score down this line, cutting through both pieces of plastic.

4. Remove the top strip of plastic that has been exposed and then peel back the other side and remove the offcut below that. When the two edges are replaced, they should meet to form a perfect straight line.

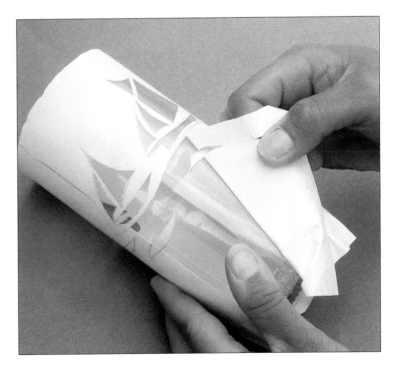

5. Draw or trace your design onto the jar or bottle, ensuring that the design forms a continuous frieze.

6. Cut the outlines of the design with a sharp knife and peel off any areas that you want to etch. (Really concentrate while you are doing this, otherwise you may find that you have peeled off the wrong areas.)

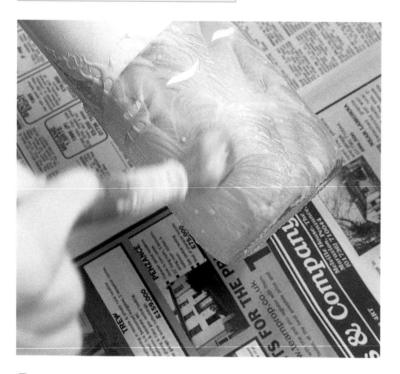

7. Place the jar or bottle on plenty of newspaper in a well-ventilated area. Wearing rubber gloves, place one hand inside the jar or bottle so that you can grip and move it without touching the outside. Start laying the etching paste onto the exposed areas of the glass with the hogs-hair brush, and once you have applied it all, move it around at regular intervals so that the etched texture does not become patchy.

8. After about 15 minutes, fill the washing-up bowl with plenty of fresh water and wash off the etching paste with the washing-up brush, discarding the water in a safe manner when you have finished.

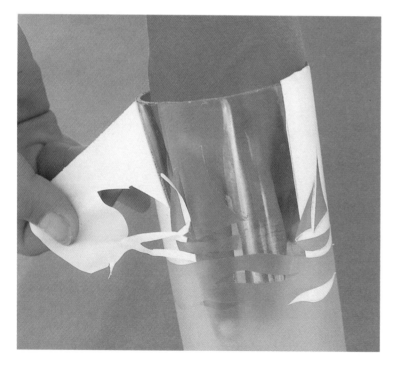

9. Thoroughly rinse the jar or bottle again before removing your rubber gloves. Peel off the sticky-back plastic.

10. The etched texture on this vase will show up best in strong sunlight, so in order to display it to its best advantage, place it on a sunny windowsill.

Decorative mirror tile with adhesive lead

This is more of a wall decoration than a mirror. It looks effective, but doesn't actually leave much space to admire oneself in, although, with luck, your friends will be admiring your handiwork rather than themselves.

Equipment and Materials
sheet of sticky-back plastic
30.5 centimetre (12 inch) square
mirror tile
small, sharp craft knife
soft cloth or paper towels
soft and sharp pencils
a template of the design
sticky tape
white spirit
newspaper
rubber gloves
etching paste
chunky, hogs-hair paintbrush and
plastic container to hold it
old washing-up bowl and brush
lots of fresh water
bicarbonate of soda
adhesive lead strip
sharp pair of scissors
fid
scalpel
small, soft shoe brush or old
toothbrush
graphite grate polish

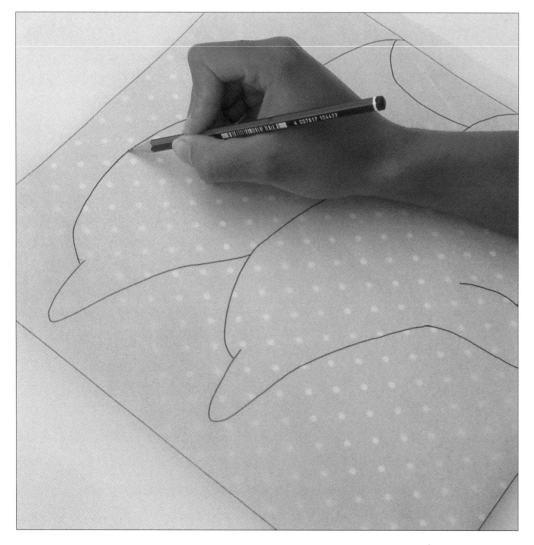

1. Apply the sticky-back plastic to the mirror tile, allowing an overlap of approximately 1.25 centimetres (½ inch) all round. Trim the plastic to the size of the mirror. Trace the design to be etched onto the plastic and cut through the outline with a sharp knife.

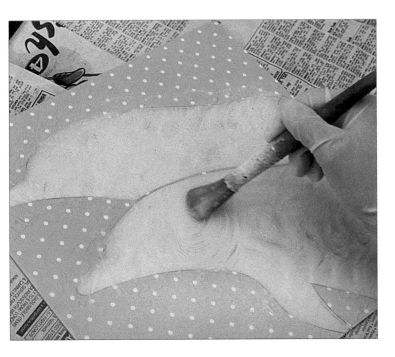

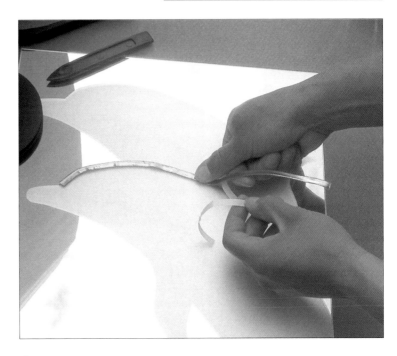

2. Peel off the plastic and prepare the area for etching. Apply the etching paste in the usual manner, ensuring that you always keep it moving, as the larger the area to be etched, the more likely it is to appear patchy when you have finished. After 15 minutes, wash off the etching paste, using plenty of water. Dry the mirror tile thoroughly and remove the sticky-back plastic.

3. Measure a length of adhesive lead which will reach from the forehead of the dolphin to the tip of its back fin, adding a little extra to be on the safe side, before cutting it with scissors. Peel off the backing paper and lay the lead strip onto the mirror, easing it gently around the curves as you go. Trim off the excess lead and, using a fid, press it onto the mirror.

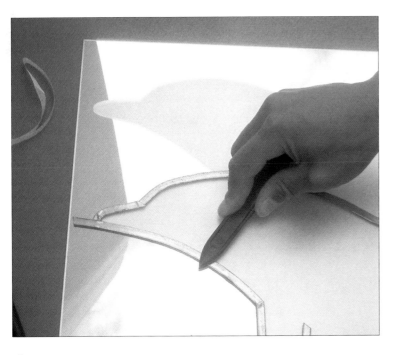

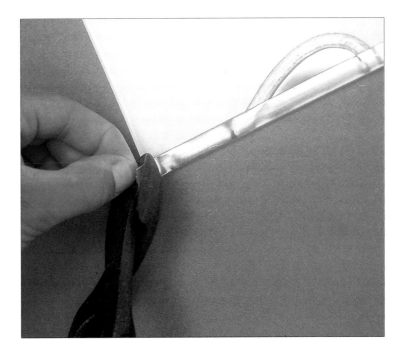

4. Cut the next length of adhesive lead so that it is long enough to reach from the dolphin's forehead to the end of its beak, cutting the adhesive lead to an angle that will abut the first piece. Now repeat the process outlined in step 3. Continue in this way until you have outlined both dolphins with the adhesive lead.

5. Apply a further strip of adhesive lead around the perimeter of the mirror so that the edges are completely hidden. This will make the tile look as though it has been framed.

6. Cut a piece of sticky-back plastic large enough to cover the etched area of the top dolphin and then stick it down.

7. Using your fingernail or a blunt pencil, press hard against the edge of the lead so that the plastic is sufficiently indented to act as a cutting guide.

8. Using a scalpel, cut around the outside.

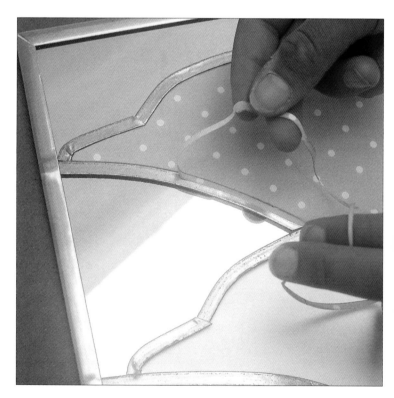

9. Peel off any excess plastic.

10. Using a shoe brush or an old toothbrush, apply enough grate polish to the lead and the etched area of the second dolphin to cover them. Working in a circular motion, keep rubbing the polish with the brush until it has been absorbed into the surface of the lead and etched mirror.

11. Give it 4 or 5 minutes, and then, using a soft cloth, paper towels or another clean soft brush, polish the blackened areas thoroughly to bring out the shine of the graphite.

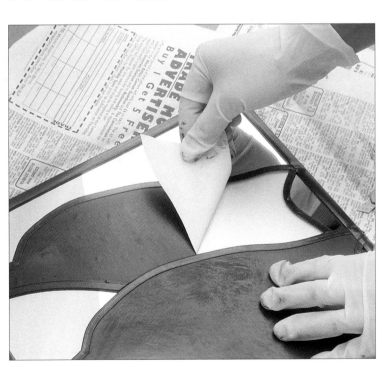

12. Carefully remove the plastic, taking care not to get any of the polish on the white, etched area, as it is difficult to clean off (if you do, however, remove it with white spirit). Because grate polish is oil-based, it may come off on your hands for a few days after application, so leave it to dry for a couple of days before mounting it.

13. The mirror tile can be attached to the wall with the double-sided adhesive pads that the manufacturer usually supplies with it.

CHAPTER 5
Glass cutting

Mosaic mirror

This mosaic-framed mirror does not require foiling and consists of straight-edged pieces, so it is an ideal first project for glass cutting. Unlike true mosaic tesserae, which can be cut with a clipper-like tool, stained-glass tesserae must be cut with an ordinary glasscutter to avoid them shattering and covering you with dangerous shards. It is also easier to design an item that includes larger pieces of glass, which are more manageable.

Equipment and Materials

saw
dust mask
1 piece MDF or chipboard for an eventual size 40.6 centimetres (16 inches) square
3 pieces opalescent glass of different colours
glasscutter
pencil
straightedge
stiff card
scissors
breaking pliers
carborundum stone or grinder
1 mirror tile 30.5 centimetres (12 inches) square
tile cement and spreader
piece of thin paper
flat board
cloths for cleaning
grout (optional)
fine sandpaper
bradawl
2 screw eyes
chain or cord for hanging

1. Wearing a dusk mask and using a saw, cut a piece of MDF or chipboard 40.6 centimetres (16 inches) square to accommodate the mirror and mosaic tiles around it.

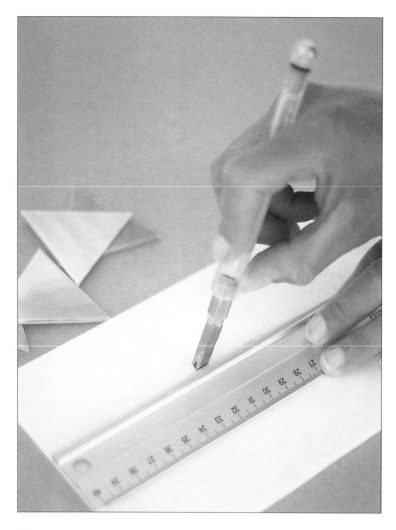

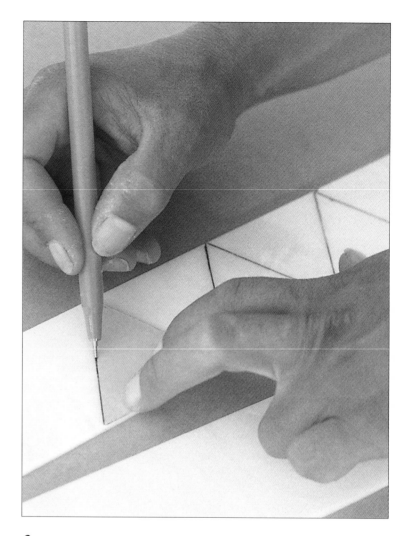

2. Equilateral triangles of coloured glass are used to make the design for the frame. The easiest way to cut these is, using a glasscutter, first to cut a strip of glass 5 centimetres (2 inches) wide from a sheet of coloured glass. Having chosen green, white and blue, I cut two strips of white glass approximately 35.5 centimetres (14 inches) long, and one each of green and blue glass of the same length.

You will find it helpful to draw a line on the glass to guide you and to cut the glass using a straightedge. When the wheel of the glasscutter is positioned on the line, the straightedge should be about 3 millimetres (1/8 inch) away from it to accommodate the width of the glasscutter's head. Place the glasscutter at the far edge of the glass and then, holding the straightedge firmly, pull the glasscutter towards you to the near side of the glass. (If you are using an oil-filled glasscutter, you will notice that the head appears to wobble – this is to prevent the glasscutter from wandering away from the straightedge when you are cutting the glass. If you are using an ordinary glasscutter, you will have to take care that this does not happen.)

3. Using the drawing in this book, make a template from stiff card and cut it out. Place the template on the glass and draw around it to mark the outlines of each of the tesserae. The individual triangles can be scored either freehand or against a straightedge, whichever you find the easiest. Once you have scored it, break off each tessera triangle with either your hands or breaking pliers. You will need to cut 20 white triangles, 12 blue and 12 green triangles. You will also need to cut four white tesserae to a different shape, as given in this book.

If all of these tesserae break cleanly, you will have to do very little to them, but if they have sharp or uneven edges, you will have to rub them down gently with a wet carborundum stone, or, if you have one, a grinder.

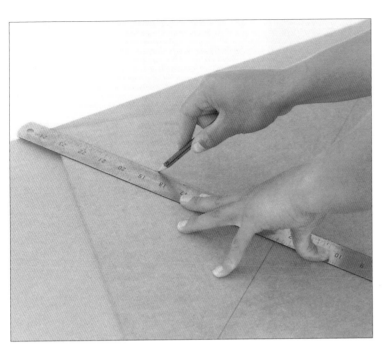

4. To centre the mirror tile on the MDF or chipboard, using a straightedge and pencil, draw diagonal lines across the board from each corner so that they cross in the middle. The diagonals should intersect the corners of the mirror tile when it is placed in the right position. Ensure that the mirror tile and glass tesserae are clean and grease-free.

5. Place a good-sized dollop of tile cement in the middle of the MDF or chipboard and spread it out using the spreader that should have been supplied with the cement.

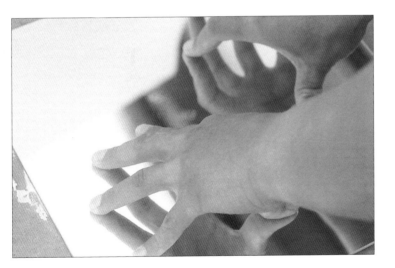

6. Press the mirror tile firmly into the cement, ensuring that its corners line up with the diagonals. The cement should ooze out from under the edges of the mirror tile.

7. Apply more cement around the edge of the mirror tile and then arrange the tesserae on it, starting with the white triangles, which should fit exactly along the edge of the mirror. Now position the coloured triangles between the white triangles. The last tiles to be positioned are the corner pieces. The cement should ooze up between the tesserae a little.

To ensure that the tiles are level, place a piece of thin paper over the whole mirror and a flat board on top of that. Press down on the board gently and evenly to level the tiles and prevent any sharp edges from sticking up.

8. Remove the board and peel off the paper carefully before gently wiping off any excess cement from the surface of the mirror and tesserae. Leave the cement to set for the time indicated by the manufacturer.

When the cement is dry, polish the mirror to remove any residue before applying more cement or grout to any gaps between the tesserae. Leave the grout for 15 minutes and then wipe the work clean.

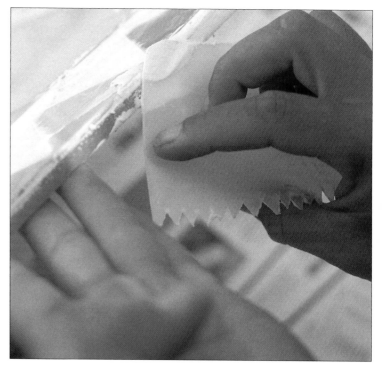

9. To dull any sharp edges around the perimeter, coat the edges of the mirror with a generous layer of cement or grout and then leave it to dry.

10. When your work is dry, gently rub it down with some fine sandpaper.

Turn the mirror over and measure two points an equal distance from the top on each side. Use a bradawl, mark these points with a small hole and attach a screw eye to each hole. String a chain or cord through the screw eyes to enable the mirror to be hung.

Twig or driftwood mobile

When buying stained glass, it is often possible to obtain offcuts, which are sold by weight. For this mobile, I have made all of the pieces a regular shape, but different sizes. If you prefer, however, you could opt for completely different shapes or use untrimmed offcuts. By hanging the individual pieces close together, different colours will be obtained where they overlap. The glass is tougher than you might expect, and unless a force 8 gale is forecast, the mobile should be safe to leave outside. The mobile can either be displayed as a purely decoratively ornament, or, if it is hung outside or in an open window, can serve as a wind chime.

Equipment and Materials
4 or 5 different-coloured glass offcuts
glasscutter
breaking pliers
grinder or carborundum stone
plain copper foil
foiler
soldering board
flux
soldering iron
solder
paper towels
4 or 5 small copper rings
G-cramp
piece of driftwood or decoratively shaped twig
workbench
drill with a small-sized bit
length of nylon fishing line

1. If you are intending to cut your glass offcuts to shape, the easiest way to do this is to place each piece of glass on the pattern and then to trim it by hand using a glasscutter and breaking pliers.

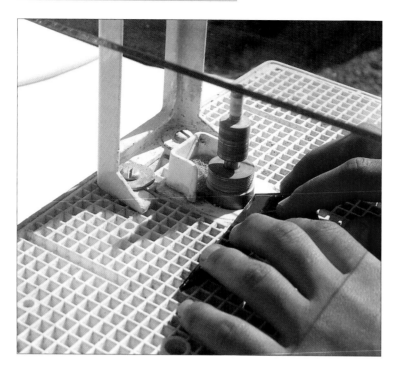

2. It is best to remove any rough edges on the glass with a grinder, so that when you foil them you won't cut either your fingers or the copper foil. (A carborundum stone will do the same job, but will take much longer.) Wash all of the glass pieces in very hot water and ensure that they are thoroughly dry.

3. Having made sure that your hands are clean, grease-free and dry, apply the copper foil to each piece of glass in turn (see page 31).

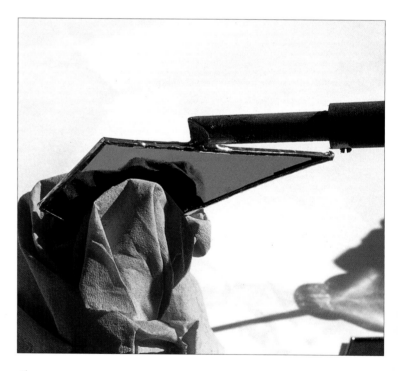

4. When you have foiled all of the pieces of glass, place them on a soldering board, flux them liberally and tin around the edges. Turn each over, flux the other side and repeat the tinning process.

5. Apply more solder to the outer edges of each piece of glass. (Remember to protect your hand with a paper towel when you are holding the glass.) To strengthen the finished piece, lay on as much solder as you can without it running or dripping off.

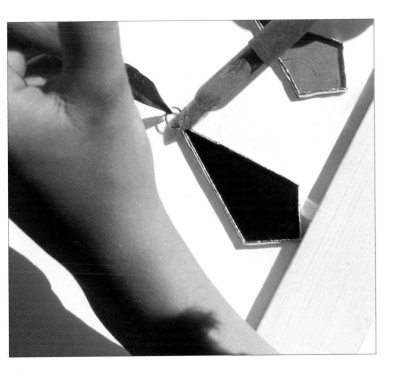

6. When you have obscured the copper foil on all of the pieces, and have applied sufficient solder to enable you to round off all of the square edges, attach a copper ring to the top of each shape. Thoroughly wash and dry each piece.

7. Using a G-clamp, secure the piece of driftwood or twig to a workbench. With a small-diameter drill bit, drill a line of holes. The space of the gaps between the holes will depend on the size of your glass pieces, as well as the amount of overlap required. Drill another hole at each end of the top edge of the driftwood or twig from which to suspend your mobile.

8. Using nylon fishing line cut to the required lengths, hang each piece of glass from the driftwood or twig at slightly different heights. Make a hanging loop through the top two holes with the same type of line.

Fish suncatcher

These simple little fish look very jolly when hung in a bathroom window. You could also make batches of different-coloured fish into a mobile and hang them in direct sunlight, causing their colours to flicker all around the room.

Equipment and Materials
2 or 3 colours of transparent glass
glasscutter
breaking pliers
grinder or carborundum stone
plain copper foil
foiler
soldering board
flux
soldering iron
solder
paper towel
1 copper ring
black glass paint and fine brush or
permanent paint marker

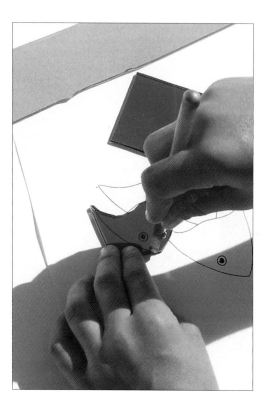

1. Using a glasscutter and breaking pliers, cut four pieces of glass and then trim them by hand.

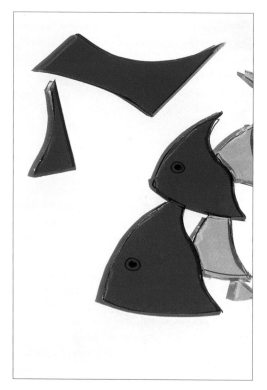

2. Grind, wash and foil all of the pieces. Arrange them together on the soldering board and flux them. Ensure that all of the pieces are in their exact positions before tack-soldering them together.

3. Once you have tacked them together, tin around the outer edges of the pieces with a small amount of solder. Now build up the bead between the body of each fish and its tail, as well as the joints between the two fishes. Turn the work over and repeat the process on the other side, not forgetting to flux it.

4. Holding the suncatcher upright, flux the tinned edges and lay some solder along them, keeping each horizontal. Because some of the edges are curved and the molten solder will run off them, you may find this more difficult than for the mobile. It is therefore easier to hold the soldering iron still in one hand, while carefully tilting the suncatcher with the other. This will keep the edge of the suncatcher that is directly below the soldering iron horizontal.

5. Don't forget to solder the exposed edges of the little triangle between the two fishes, as well as the outside edges.

6. To find the point of balance from which to suspend the fish, pick it up between your finger and thumb (take care, however, because it will now be hot and oily). When it is hanging in a good vertical position, you are holding the point of balance.

7. Fix the copper ring to the point of balance and then wash and dry the suncatcher.

8. Place the suncatcher on the pattern in this book, and then, using either black glass paint and a fine brush or permanent paint marker, trace the eye onto the glass.

Your work of art is now ready to be displayed.

Sailing boat on a stand

Instead of hanging in the window, this little boat is designed to stand on the windowsill. You could also make it from opalescent, rather than transparent, glass and display it in a cabinet. Once you have got the hang of this very simple version, you could design some more elaborate craft with different sail patterns to create your own miniature fleet.

Equipment and Materials
template p118
2 or 3 pieces different-coloured
transparent glass
glasscutter
breaking pliers
card
fine pen
1 piece opalescent glass
grinder or carborundum stone
($^7/_{32}$ inch) and ($^1/_4$ inch) copper foil
foiler
soldering board
flux
soldering iron
solder
about 20 centimetres (8 inches)
copper wire
small pair of pliers
paper towel
ice-cream box or similar filled with
screwed-up newspaper
black glass paint and fine brush
(optional)

1. First cut out the glass pieces for the transparent parts of the boat, using the design given in this book. You will need to make a template out of card to draw around when cutting out the base, as you will not be able see the outline of the pattern through the opalescent glass. Outline the pattern pieces on the opaque glass using a fine pen, and then cut it in the same way as the transparent glass. (You may find that opalescent glass is harder to cut because the white substance that makes the glass opaque also makes it harder. In addition, when you come to break the glass after having scored it, while you can see that the score line has cracked on transparent glass, you can't on opaque glass, and will either have to trust your senses, or, after a little practice, judge whether or not it has cracked by the tone that it made while you were scoring it.)

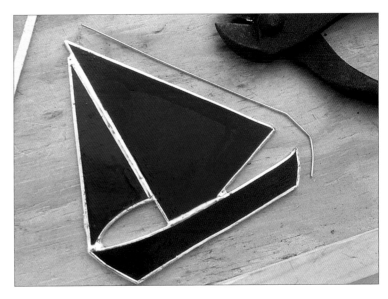

2. Grind, wash and then dry the five pieces of glass before foiling them. For both the hull and sails, the ⁷/₃₂ inch foil is sufficient. Because it is a three-dimensional object, however, it is safer to use a slightly wider foil around the base pieces, and I recommend ¹/₄ inch foil. Place the three transparent pieces of the boat on the soldering board and flux them generously. Tack the pieces together.

3. Cut a length of copper wire long enough to reach from the top of the large sail to the bottom of the hull. You will need to make two slight bends in the wire with some small pliers: one where it leaves the sail and one where it joins the top of the stern to follow the angle of the edge. Now flux the wire and tack-solder it to the outside foil of these two pieces.

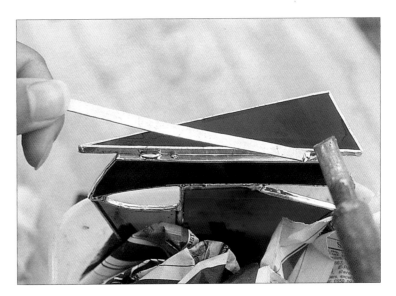

4. Using slightly more solder on the edges incorporating the wire, tin around the shape. Now build up the bead down the mast and along where the sail meets the hull. Turn the boat over, flux the other side and repeat the process.

When you come to build up the solder around the outside edge, lay it over both the copper wire and the foil to make the outside of this edge appear as though it has just been soldered rather more thickly. Although it conveniently happens to look like a rigging rope, the wire is there to brace the boat, which is slightly weak at the point between the sail and hull, and the straight line may weaken and bend with constant handling.

5. Once you have completed the two-dimensional shape of the boat, turn it upside down and place it on the newspaper in the ice-cream box. (This will help to support the boat, leaving both of your hands free to tack on the base pieces.) Flux the bottom of the boat again, as well as the foil on the base pieces. Tack the first base piece to the bottom of the boat, making sure that the pointed end faces the bow of the boat (otherwise the boat will appear to be sailing backwards). It should be tacked corner edge to corner edge so that the pieces do not overlap.

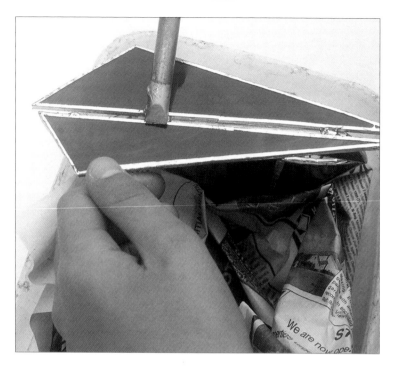

6. Turn the box around and tack on the second base piece, again edge to edge. A 'U'-shaped channel will be left between the two base pieces, with the bottom of the boat's hull as the bottom of the channel. Carefully remove the boat from the box and stand it on its base, the right way up.

7. Flux the copper foil in the right angle made between the boat and the base and then lay a little bead of solder along this angle, from one end of the hull to the other. Repeat the process on the other side of the boat and then fill the gap between the two halves of the base behind the hull with solder.

8. Turn the boat upside down and return it to the newspaper-filled box. Now fill the channel with solder. This time the solder bead must be left as flat as possible, and not raised, otherwise the boat will wobble when it is placed on a flat surface.

9. Flux the outer edges of the base, and then, holding the boat by its sail, lay solder along these straight edges to finish off your work.

10. Carefully wash and dry the boat. If you like, you could paint a registration number on the sail using black glass paint and a fine brush. Your little craft is now ready for launching on a sunny windowsill.

Holly wreath

With a candle in the centre, this wreath would make an ideal table decoration for Christmas. You could also hang it from a securely attached door hook. With a little imagination, you could adapt the design to create a fruit or floral garland, or maybe even one incorporating swimming fish. Have a doodle: you may surprise yourself!

Equipment and Materials
template p119
green glass
orange or red glass (you could use orange or red glass nuggets for the berries)
glasscutter
breaking pliers
grinder
(³/₈ inch) plain copper foil
foiler
soldering board
flux
soldering iron
solder
paper towel
copper wire
large marker pen or (³/₄ inch) dowel

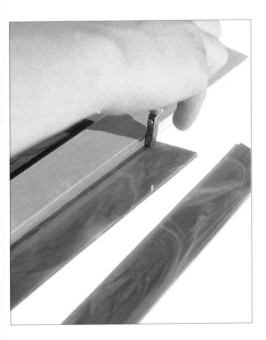

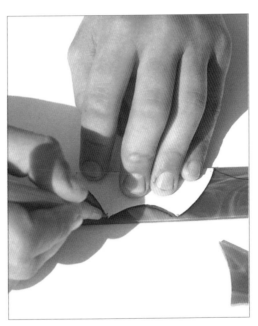

1. Cut a strip of green glass 3 centimetres (about 1¹/₂ inches) wide and about 60 centimetres (24 inches) long and a strip of orange or red glass 2 centimetres (about ³/₄ inch) by 12 centimetres (4³/₄ inches).

2. Using the leaf template given in this book, draw the holly leaves onto the strip of green glass, turning over the template after you have completed each (by doing this, the leaves will interlock, leaving little waste). This should give you six half leaves facing one way and six facing the other.

3. Cut the orange glass into pieces 2 centimetres (³/₄ inch) square, as shown on the template. Using breaking pliers, score and clip off the corners of each, so that you are left with octagons.

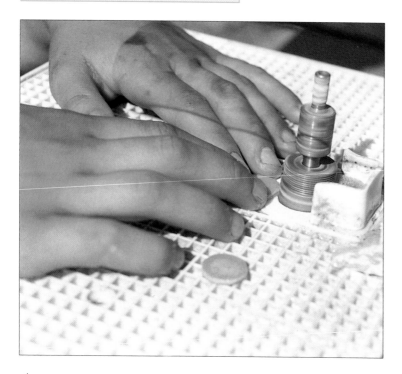

4. Using a grinder, round off the points of the octagons to form circles, and also neaten up the leaves.

5. Wash all of the glass pieces in boiling water and dry them. Now foil the pieces with (¹/₂ inch) copper foil. Pair up the sets of half leaves so that the right-hand side is offset slightly forward from the left-hand side. This will enable you to key up the leaves more easily when you are making the wreath.

6. Tack-solder the halves together to make up the individual leaves.

7. Solder both of the sides and all of the edges of the leaves. Tin and build up a solder bead on the berries (these are very small, so take care not to burn your fingers on the soldering iron).

8. Arrange the leaves in a circle, as shown, and tack-solder them together.

9. Tack-solder the berries onto the central spine of each leaf, in the position shown.

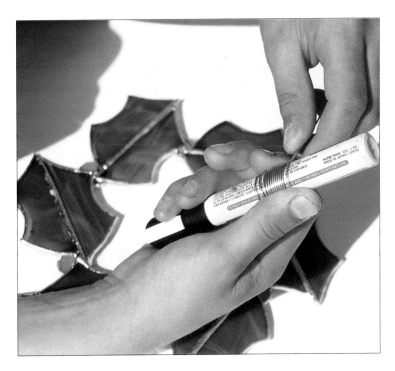

10. Holding the wreath vertical, tack-solder the berries at other points to ensure that they are secure. Turn the wreath upside down and touch up the tack points on the underside.

11. Wind a length of copper wire around a large marker pen or 1.9 centimetre (³/₄ inch) dowel 13 or 14 times.

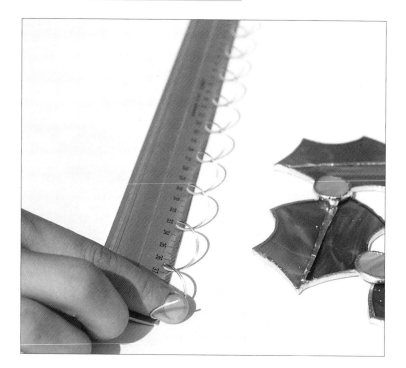

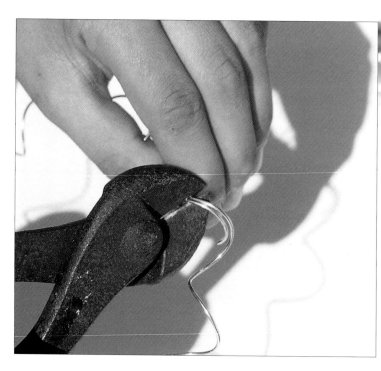

12. Remove the pen or dowel, and, holding the ends of the wire, pull them outwards until 12 revolutions stretch to a length of 46 centimetres (about 18 inches).

13. Form the wire into a circle and overlap the ends so that you have a loop of wire that consists of these 12 revolutions. Cut off the excess wire as shown.

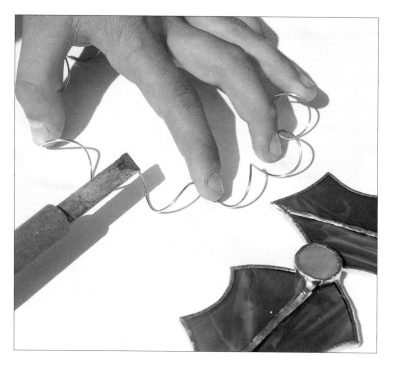

14. Flux and solder the ends together.

15. Place the wire circle on the base of the wreath. There should be two revolutions per leaf, so tack every alternate revolution to the same position on a leaf. The wire circle will act as a stand if you want to use the wreath as a centrepiece and is also secure enough to hang from a door as a garland.

Terrarium

This terrarium is more complicated to construct than a two-dimensional object because there is no base board to retain the solder, which means that it tends to trickle between the joints. It may therefore be necessary to stuff the terrarium with screwed-up newspaper or to stick some masking tape to the back of the joints while you are soldering them. Three-dimensional projects have a habit of collecting more solder on the board beneath the work in progress than on the work itself, so it is fortunate that the solder can be melted and used again.

Equipment and Materials
template p124
3 different colours opalescent glass
3 millimetre ($^1/_8$ inch) clear glass
3 millimetre ($^1/_8$ inch)
mirror glass
stiff card
glasscutter
breaking pliers
grinder
22 millimetre ($^7/_8$ inch) copper,
black- and silver-backed foil
foiler
straightedge
soldering board
flux
soldering iron
solder
paper towel
large container filled with
screwed-up newspaper
or blocks of wood
masking tape
copper wire

1. Cut out all of the pieces of glass according to the pattern in the book. In the case of the opaque glass, transfer the pattern to stiff card, place the card on the glass and draw around it. Now foil the pieces of glass. When foiling the transparent pieces, use black-backed foil rather than ordinary copper foil, as the adhesive side of the foil will be visible through the glass and will appear coppered when the solder is applied to the joints. For the same reason, use silver-backed foil for the mirrored backplate. Next, make up the individual flat panels of the terrarium. Lay the individual pieces of the first panel together, with their sides lined up against a straightedge, and tack-solder them together at two points on each joint.

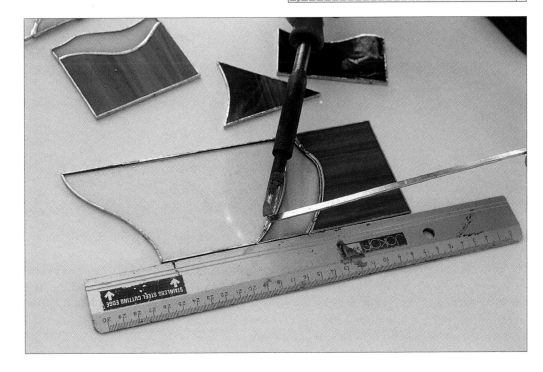

85

2. Tin around the outer edge of the whole panel, then build up beads of solder along the lines where you first tacked. Simply tin any pieces that will not be tacked to others, such as the mirrored backplate and base.

3. After tinning them, carefully hold the mirrored backplate and base together, corner to corner, and then tack-solder them.

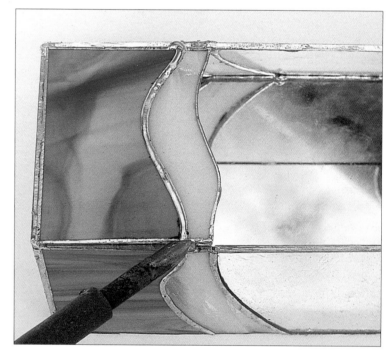

4. Turn these two pieces on their sides, so that a right angle is facing you, making it easier to tack-solder the side panel to both the back panel and the base panel in the same way. (You may need to support it slightly so that it doesn't tip forwards.) Turn your work over, and tack-solder the other side panel.

5. Lay your work onto its mirrored backplate and then tack the upper and lower front panels to the sides and base, ensuring that the top corners of the upper panel meet the corners of the side pieces accurately.

6. Tack-solder the coloured roof panel to both the top front panel and the mirrored back panel and then tack-solder the triangular side panels into the corners. If your cutting has been accurate, everything should fit together, but it is possible that there will be gaps between the panels through which the solder will drip. Bearing in mind that the solder is liquid when it is molten, each of these joints should now be soldered horizontally, with each side sloping downwards at an equal angle and the top joint level. You can do this either by supporting your work with a fairly large box filled with screwed-up newspaper or by using blocks of wood to support it at various angles while you are soldering each joint. If they are accessible, it is helpful to cover the inside joints with masking tape or to stuff screwed-up newspaper into the terrarium, as it will not be easy to remove any drops of solder that have leaked through should they have fallen on, and stuck to, an internal soldered joint.

7. Before soldering the joints between the small top triangles and the mirrored backplate, you need to insert a length of copper wire into the channel of this joint and embed it well with solder. Cut a length of copper wire long enough to embed it at least 2.5 centimetres (1 inch) into the channel on each side and then create a loop above it to hang the terrarium from. Now tack-solder one end of the wire into the channel created by the backplate and the side triangle. Bend the wire into an arc above it, and then tack-solder the other end into the channel on the opposite side.

8. When you have soldered this bead, the wire should be set well enough into the solder to prevent the foil from pulling away from the glass due to the weight of the terrarium and its contents.

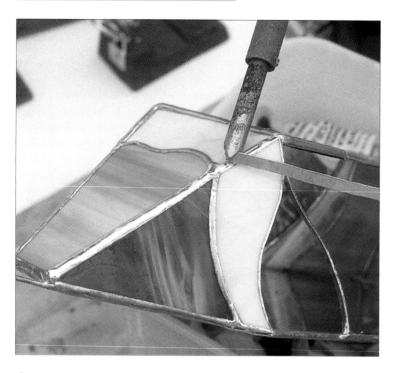

9. Check to make sure that you haven't forgotten to solder any joints.

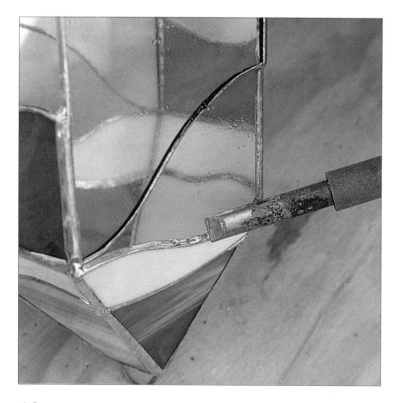

10. Carefully wash and dry your terrarium. You could now fill it with a thin layer of grit, plenty of soil and some suitable plants, such as ivy, tradescantia and other small, trailing plants. It is not suitable for cut flowers in standing water, however, as the joints between the foil and the glass are not 100 per cent watertight.

Lampshade

I have kept the design and construction of this lampshade simple for two reasons. Firstly, I think that much American-made glass is so attractive that it seems a shame to cut it into such small pieces that its beauty is lost. Secondly, a form over which to create the shade is required for many of the very intricate designs, which you may use only once and which will add to the overall cost of your lamp. The only support needed for this simple, six-sided shade is a couple of different-sized offcuts of timber and a box of screwed-up newspaper. The lampshade is suitable for hanging from the ceiling or for a small bedside or standard lamp.

Equipment and Materials
template p120
3 different-coloured pieces of opalescent glass
glasscutter
breaking pliers
grinder
waterproof marker pen
22 millimetre ($^7/_{32}$ inch) copper foil
foiler
straightedge
soldering board
flux
soldering iron
solder
paper towel
large container filled with screwed-up newspaper or board with a batten right angle
vase cap
masking tape (optional)
patina (optional)
either a lamp base and brass fittings (finial, harp, bulb-holder, three-core flex and plug) or brass fittings for a hanging shade (2.5 centimetre (1 inch) threaded tube, hanging ring, chain, ceiling rose with hook, bulb-holder and three-core flex)

1. Using the pattern in this book, cut the 18 pieces of glass needed for the shade, 6 shapes from each piece of coloured glass.

2. The most effective, and least wasteful, way to cut the largest pieces of glass for the main body of the lampshade is to interlock them, one facing upwards and one facing downwards.

3. The individual panel pieces must fit together snugly, so when you are grinding them to fit each other, it is helpful to number the three pieces of each side with a waterproof marker pen, so that when you make up each panel you can be certain that the pieces you ground to fit are the same pieces that you are soldering together.

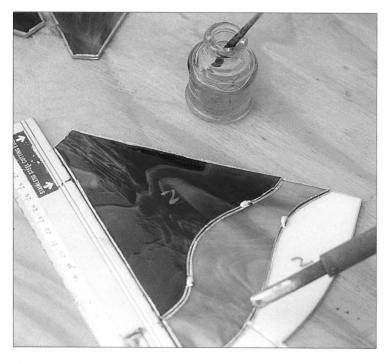

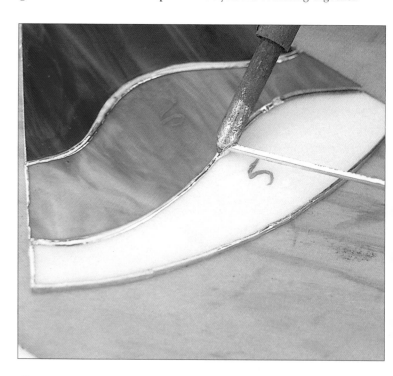

4. Once you have ground and washed all of the pieces, foil them with (7/32 inch) copper foil. Now tack-solder the individual pieces together to make up six separate panels, each consisting of three pieces. Use a straight edge to align the pieces.

5. Build up a bead of solder between these pieces on both sides. Now lightly tin around the edge of each panel, making sure that there are not too many overruns of solder on the outside edges which would prevent the panels from fitting together closely.

6. These individual panels should now be tack-soldered together. There are several ways of doing this. I find that working on a board with a batten right angle in one corner, against which the bottom edge of the pieces can be supported, is the easiest. However you may find it better either to lay the first panel flat, right side down, and then to tack-solder the second panel onto it from the inside, or else to support it in a box of rolled-up newspaper.

7. Whichever you prefer, you must ensure that you tack-solder the top corners of each panel accurately, so that when you come to fit the last panel, it lines up with the first one snugly.

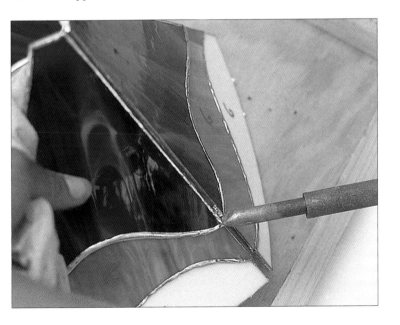

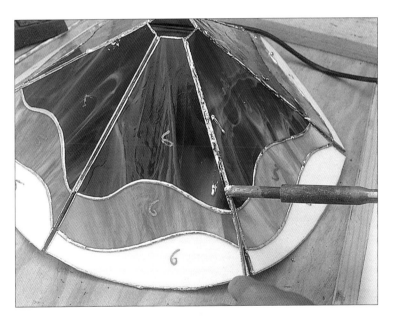

8. You must also tack-solder each panel near the bottom to hold the structure rigid, making sure that there is as little a gap as possible between the panels. Because the weight of the glass is considerable, if you are not gentle enough when doing this, it is quite easy to pull the copper foil away from the sections while you are tack-soldering them together. If this should happen to you, wash and dry all of the pieces thoroughly before foiling over the section that you have pulled away.

9. Once you have tack-soldered all of the pieces in place, run a little solder down the 'V'-shaped channel between each joint to strengthen it temporarily. This doesn't have to be neat, as you will be soldering a proper bead over it later, but it will help to hold the shape of the shade at this stage.

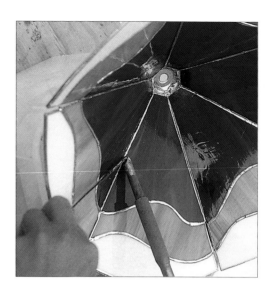

10. Invert the lampshade and place it on a hard surface with a vase cap positioned under the small hexagonal opening at the top of the shade. (The cap must be centrally positioned over this opening, and it is easier to judge the accuracy of the positioning when it is this way up.)

11. To make sure that it remains in position, drop a little tack of solder onto every other joint where it makes contact with the vase cap, and then fill in this area with a more generous amount of solder, so that the vase cap is securely sealed to the top of the lampshade. This will hold all of your pieces together in a stable hexagon while you are carrying out the rest of the soldering.

12. Build up each of the inside joints with solder. Although the solder does not need to be proud, enough should be applied to support each joint.

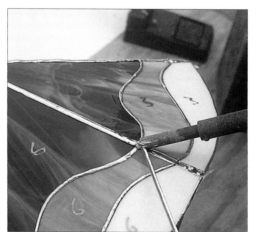

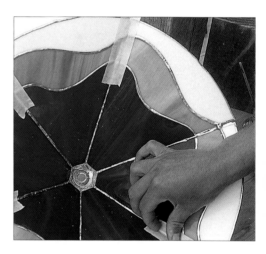

13. Turn the lampshade the right way up and support it by whatever method you find easiest, ensuring that the joint to be soldered is level.

14. Start to build up the external joints. Each of these must be exactly horizontal to the base board, otherwise the solder will either run off or blob at one end. If your cutting is not 100 per cent accurate – and it rarely is – you must somehow prevent the solder from trickling through.

15. You could stick some masking tape to the inside of each joint to support the inside bead of solder that you have already applied. However, because the tape will not stick to a fluxed surface, you must gently wash and dry the lampshade thoroughly to ensure the adhesion of the tape.

You may need to go over each bead more than once because small bubbles will appear at the points where the flux boils with the heat of the iron, leaving an uneven surface.

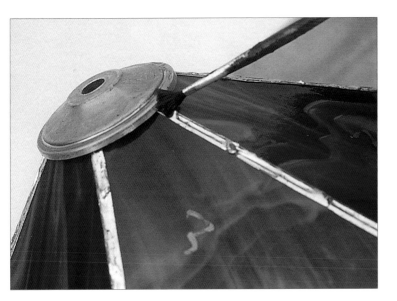

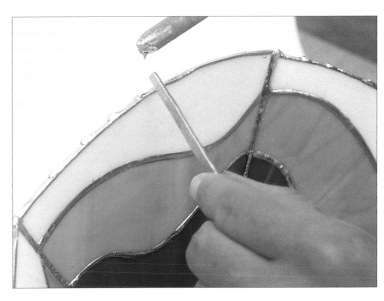

16. The outside beads of solder must also adhere to the vase cap to prevent it from pulling away from the foil around the top of the shade because of the weight of the glass. Remember that flux will help the solder to run and to make a smooth bead (but it will also sometimes spit, so make sure that you either keep it well away from your eyes or wear goggles).

17. When you have soldered all of the joints to your satisfaction, build up the foil on the lower rim of the shade with solder. Because this is a curved edge, it is easiest to leave little reservoirs of solder drops along this edge before you make a start.

18. Flux the edge and then, with the corner in contact with the foil, run the soldering iron along it, turning the shade with your other hand so that the section that you are soldering is horizontal, thus preventing the solder from running off. Remember that using the flat face of the iron will remove the solder rather than lay it on. Remove the masking tape and touch up the inside joints where some solder may have dripped through.

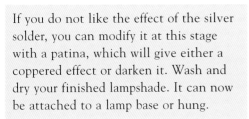

If you do not like the effect of the silver solder, you can modify it at this stage with a patina, which will give either a coppered effect or darken it. Wash and dry your finished lampshade. It can now be attached to a lamp base or hung.

19. Before attaching the lampshade to a lamp base, you will
need a harp, which has a small screw at the top which fits
through the hole in the vase cap. A finial is then screwed into
the harp to hold the shade steady. The base of the harp, which is
detachable from the sides, must be placed below the bulb-holder.
All fittings must be of brass, not plastic, and the lamp will require
a three-core flex, which is earthed. You should be able to buy
brass lamp bases with the correct fittings from most stores that
stock stained glass. You can also use a wooden base if a brass
fitting is screwed to the top to take the bulb-holder.

For a hanging shade, the bulb-holder must be screwed into a
short length of threaded tube, which is then pushed through the
hole in the vase cap and screwed into a brass hanging ring. The
lampshade can then be hung at your preferred height from a
length of chain suspended from a brass ceiling rose with a hook.
The flex must be threaded through the chain so that it does not
bear the weight of the lamp, which would be dangerous. Finally,
check all of the wiring in the plug and bulb-holder before
switching on the power, otherwise your lamp may not be the only
thing to light up!

*Right: Clockwise from top: lamp base, bulb-holder, finial,
vase cap, ceiling rose with chain, four- and three-legged
spiders, hanging ring and harp.*

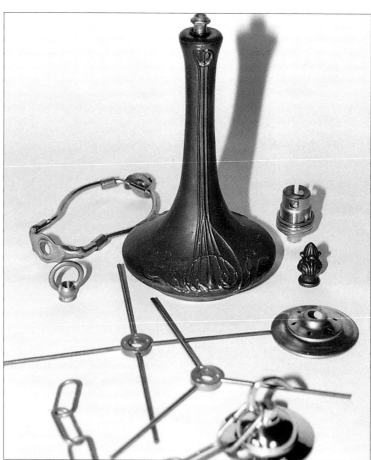

CHAPTER 6
Advanced projects

Tiffany-style painted lampshade

This project makes use of most of the techniques in this book: acid-etching, painting and cutting. It's very eco-friendly, as you can use one old jar to create a beautiful new object. It is probably the cheapest way to acquire a Tiffany-style lampshade.

Equipment and Materials
template p119
large glass jar
fine pen
boiling water
glasscutter
grinder
acid-etching equipment (see page 11)
box filled with screwed-up newspaper
outline relief paste
sharp craft knife
glass paints
paint brushes or a medicine dropper
cotton buds and white spirit (if the outline relief is gold and the glass paints are spirit-based)
four-legged spider
hacksaw
lamp base
lamp base and brass fittings (finial, 12.7 centimetre (5 inch) harp, bulb-holder, three-core flex and plug)

1. The first stage of this project is the most difficult. Fill the large glass jar with water to reach the top of the shoulder, just below the screw top. Using a fine pen, mark the water level on the glass. This is your score-line guide. Carefully score along the line. (It is not very easy at this angle, as the glasscutter wheel is inclined to slip.) Pour boiling water over the score line, being careful not to scald yourself (the water will trickle back down the underside of the jar when it is held at this angle). Hold the score line under a running cold tap and turn the vessel until the glass cracks along the score line. Pull off the top section and discard it.

2. The second cut is made lower down the bottle. Decide how deep you want the lampshade to be, bearing in mind that it has to obscure a 12.7 centimetre (5 inch) harp. The cut does not have to be a straight line, and I have made mine an undulating one.

3. Draw this line on the jar with a pen, pour boiling water over the score line and then run the jar under a cold tap until the score line cracks.

4. Grind the edges of the top and bottom cuts.

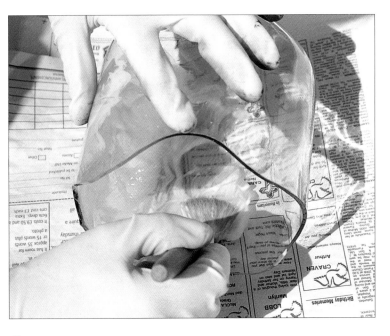

5. Using all of the recommended safety equipment (see page 11), acid-etch the inside of the lampshade. Remember to keep the acid moving to ensure a smooth and even finish. The reason for etching the inside, rather than the outside of the jar is so that when you apply the glass paint, the etched texture will not 'fill in' and become transparent again, revealing the lamp fittings

6. Wash and dry the lampshade thoroughly. Cut around the paper pattern and snip into the small nicks marked along the bottom edge. Because these tabs overlap each other, they will ensure that the pattern fits into the shoulder of the lampshade. Place the lampshade in the box of screwed-up newspaper. Using the outline relief, trace the design onto it. Remember to let each section dry thoroughly before moving the shade around to the next part, otherwise you will smudge the outline relief.

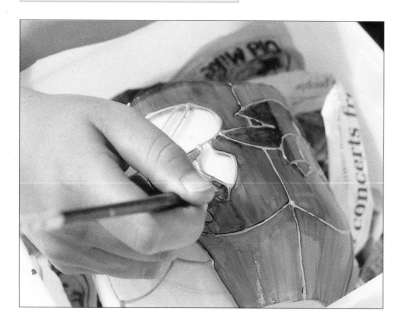

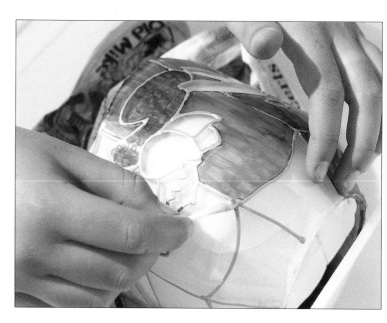

7. Once the outline relief is dry, trim off any unsightly overruns with a sharp craft knife. You can now start painting. Although it is quite difficult to keep the paint even and not leave brushstrokes, your technique will improve with practice. (You may find it easier to use a medicine dropper.) Be careful not to use too much paint, however, because since you are working on a curved surface the paint will bleed over the outline relief. Paint the whole shade, except the wings of the dragonfly, which will appear white.

8. If you are using a gold outline as I have done, (rather than black) you may need to clean the paint off it as you work. Wipe the top of the outline relief carefully with a cotton bud dipped in white spirit (assuming you are using spirit-based paint). Don't make the cotton bud too wet, as you don't want white spirit to flood into your paint and leave a pale area. An even easier way, although it's rather a cheat, is to finish painting the whole shade and then to go over the outline very carefully with a gold pen.

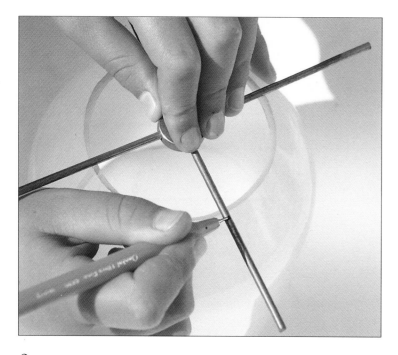

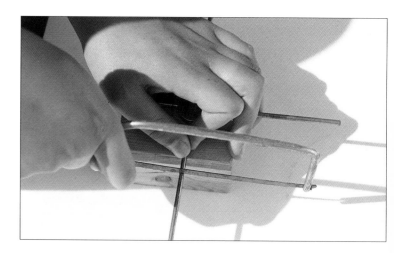

10. Using a hacksaw, cut the legs to length.

Wire up the lamp base and fit a plug. Make sure that you use three-core flex (i.e., with an earth wire). Some lamp bases have a threaded fitting on which to screw the bulb-holder, but if yours does not, fit a short length of threaded tube into the base. Remember to place the harp over this before you fit and wire the bulb-holder. At the top of the harp is a threaded spigot. Place the spider over this and screw on the finial, tightening it to hold it in position. Your Tiffany-style lampshade can now be placed so that it rests on the spider's legs.

9. Position the spider across the top of the lampshade so that the hole in it is centred with the hole in the top of the shade. Using a pen, mark a point approximately 6 millimetres (¼ inch) more than the width of the top of the lampshade on the spider's legs

Chalice

This dramatic-looking object can be used for flower arrangements, as a sports trophy or even as a bacchanalian fruit bowl. By cutting the bottle at a certain height and making the neck into the base, most bottles can be converted into some sort of trophy, and the proportions of this brandy bottle work exceptionally well. However, to paraphrase Mrs Beeton, 'First, drink your brandy!'

Equipment and Materials

bottle, preferably a brandy bottle
glasscutting equipment (see page 27)
boiling water
sheet of copper foil
sharp craft knife
($^5/_8$ inch) copper foil
fid
at least 12 glass nuggets
($^3/_8$ inch) copper foil
paper
black pen
soldering equipment
approximately 15 inches copper wire
long-nosed pliers
copper-sulphate patina
paintbrush

1. Using the technique of filling the bottle with water to just below the shoulder to ensure a straight line, mark a score line on the bottle.

2. Score and cut the bottle, using the boiling/cold-water method to separate the top and bottom (see pp 26–27).

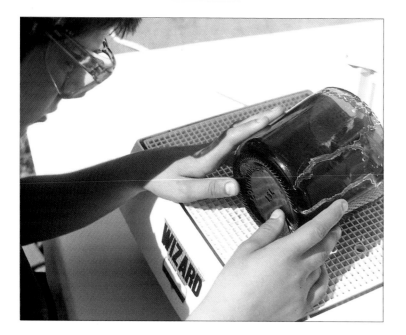

3. Grind the rough edges and then wash and dry both parts of the bottle.

4. Cut a circle of copper foil approximately 6.5 centimetres (2 ½ inches) larger all round than the base of the bottle. Now cut a length of foil to go around the top of the neck, which should be 6 millimetres (¼ inch) longer than the circumference of the neck and about 7.6 centimetres (3 inches) wide; if the neck of the bottle is tapered, ideally it should also be slightly curved.

5. Now cover the top edge of the chalice with 1.4 centimetre (⅝ inch) copper foil. Measure a length that is sufficient to go around the perimeter, to which you have added an overlap of about 1.25 centimetres (¼ inch). Peel the backing paper from the first couple of centimetres or inch of foil and place it against the outside top edge, so that less than a third of the width adheres to the edge. (Remember to leave enough to cover the horizontal plane and to overlap slightly onto the inside edge.) Continue foiling around the edge in this manner until you have overlapped the point where you started.

6. Carefully crimp the foil inwards until it covers the top edge and then crimp it again so that the remainder is on the inside. Using a fid, ensure that the foil has adhered well to all of these surfaces.

7. Wash and then foil the nuggets at this stage, too. How many you foil is up to you: do you want your chalice to be well encrusted or more subtly decorated? Use the 9 millimetre (³/₈ inch) foil for this job and again ensure that the foil overlaps and that it has adhered to the surface well.

8. Peel off the backing paper from the foil circle and position the chalice's cup section in the middle of the sticky side. Turn the chalice upside down and press the copper foil into the dip in the centre of the base, pressing it down well with a fid. Cut the foil in several places from the edge to the point at which it has adhered to the bottle.

9. Fold down the individual sections and stick them to the bottle so that they overlap each other. If necessary, and using a sharp craft knife, trim the top edge of the foil on the bottle so that you have a continuous top edge that is pleasing to the eye.

10. Peel off the backing paper from the neck section of copper foil and stick it to the bottle, ensuring that there is a good overlap at the top of the neck so that the foil goes down inside it slightly. This will ensure good adhesion when you are soldering the two halves together.

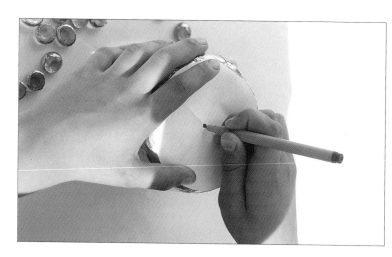

11. Make sure that all of the copper foil adheres to the glass well and that there are no air bubbles. Should you find one, pierce it with a craft knife and then press it flat.

12. You will now need to attach the base of the goblet to the cup. It must, be centrally positioned, and the easiest way to find the centre of the cup is to take a circle of paper the same size as the base, fold it in half, in half again, and then to unfold it and place it on the base. Make a hole in the centre of the paper where the two folds intersect. When the top of the base is placed upside down over it you can see this spot by looking through the original neck of the bottle. It is much easier to align the point in of this small circle.

13. Flux and tack-solder the base to the cup. Cut three pieces of copper wire approximately 10 centimetres (4 inches) long and bend each one in the middle to make a right angle. Position the lengths of copper wire so that they are aligned with both the neck of the bottle and the base of the cup and, using a pair of long-nosed pliers, add more angles to match the profile of the bottle's neck.

14. Ensure that the copper wires are evenly spaced around the neck and then tack-solder each one into position.

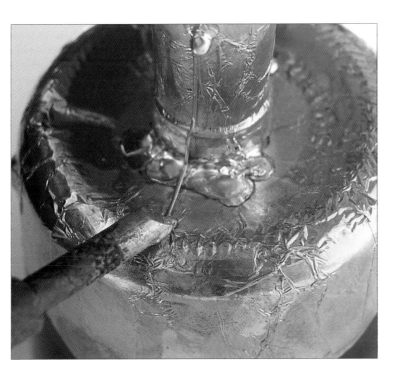

15. Cover the whole foil area in solder, encasing the strengthening wires until they have been obscured.

16. Because it is never possible to make the surface of the solder smooth, I have applied it spot by spot. This ensures that there is a sufficiently thick layer of solder and also gives it a hammered effect.

17. Flux the foil around the top edge of the chalice and apply a generous layer to the outer, inner and top surfaces. You may need to flux and melt the solder again to obtain a smooth finish. If so, move the soldering iron slowly enough to allow all of the solder in one area at a time to melt, otherwise it will drag and leave a sharp, uneven surface.

18. Flux and tin the copper foil around each of the nuggets.

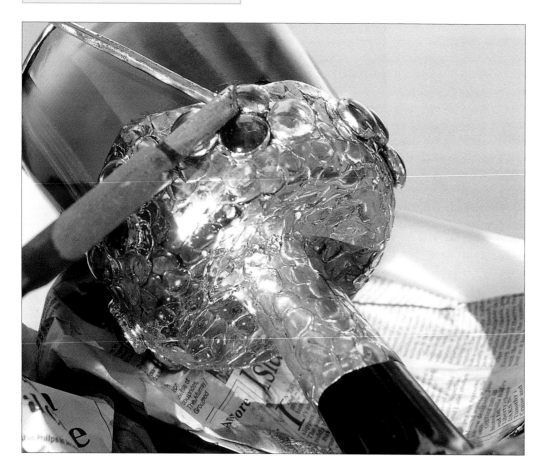

19. How you group the nuggets on the chalice is up to you, but it is advisable to tack-solder them first, in case you later change your mind. Once you are happy with your arrangement, build up the solder around each nugget until no gap is left under which the patina could later seep.

20. Wash the chalice thoroughly, paint it with copper-sulphate patina and then wash it again. The patina will give the effect of hammered copper set with jewels – a piece worthy of King Arthur.

Leaded light

We now turn to the traditional method of making stained-glass windows. Leaded lights have a framework of pure lead, which is sold in cames approximately 2 metres (6¹/₂ feet) long. The lead is 'H'-shaped in section, and the pieces of glass slot into the channels on either side. Only the joints at which these cames meet are soldered.

I have designed a simple bird motif for this project, which you could frame and hang, although a weather-proof leaded light would normally be fitted into an existing window frame. Once you have completed this practice window, you may be tempted to design your own panel to fit an aperture in your home. If so, keep your design simple and recognise your glasscutting limitations. Although lead is more forgiving when it comes to hiding bad glass cutting than copper foil, it will not hide every mistake, and you don't want the rain coming through your finished window.

Unlike making a panel using the foil technique, a gap has to be left between the pieces of glass when you are cutting them in order to accommodate the heart of the lead in the finished panel. Because this heart is 1.2 millimetres (about ¹/₁₆ inch) wide, this thickness of line must be used when you are drawing out the design from which you will cut your glass. The more accurately you cut the glass, the more easily the pieces of your panel will fit together.

Equipment and Materials
3 different-coloured pieces transparent glass
glasscutting tools (see page 12-13)
permanent marker pen
grinder
MDF board or plywood to make a glazing board
2 wooden battens 5 x 2.5 centimetres (2 x 1 inch)
dust mask
screws and screwdriver
1 came 12 millimetre (⁵/₈ inch) flat lead
2 cames 7 millimetre (³/₈ inch) oval lead
rubber gloves or barrier cream
cleat or lead clamp
work bench
pliers
lead knife
fid or oyster knife
masking tape
hammer
horseshoe nails
small brass wire brush
tallow candle
soldering iron
solder
leaded-light cement
small scrubbing brush or vegetable brush
sawdust
soft- to medium-bristle brush
grate polish
2 soft shoe brushes

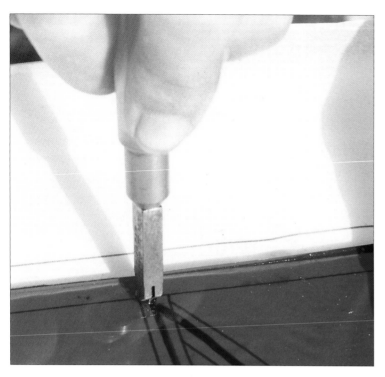

1. Lay each coloured sheet of glass on the cut-line drawing and cut it to the exact size of the white area, leaving the black outline uncovered. The pieces are numbered on the cut-line drawing, and each time you cut a piece of glass, write its number on it with a permanent marker pen and cross off the corresponding number on the drawing. This will help you to keep track of the pieces that you have cut and will also enable you to identify where they fit in the design. Although this technique is not that crucial for a window of this limited scale, if you are making a large window consisting of 30 or 40 pieces, you will be faced with a frustrating jigsaw puzzle if you have not numbered your pieces. Once you have cut all of the pieces of glass, position them on the cut-line drawing to check that the gaps between the pieces are regular and as close to the 1.2 mm (about 1/16 inch) width as possible. Grind any rough edges or pieces that you have not quite cut to the correct shape and then wash them.

2. Before creating the window panel, you will need to make a glazing board on which to work. To make up this board, use a piece of plywood or MDF board cut at least 10 centimetres (about 4 inches) larger all round than your window design. (Remember to wear a dust mask when cutting the board.) Screw down two pieces of wooden batten to form an exact right angle in one corner. This will hold the panel square and give a firm edge against which to push when you are seating the pieces of glass into the lead-came channels.

Two types of lead came are used in this panel. The one used for the panel's outside edge is 12 millimetre (⁵/₈ inch) flat lead, while the one used for the internal leadwork is 7 millimetre (³/₈ inch) oval lead. The sections of these lead types are slightly different: the flat lead has a leaf that is of an even thickness right across it, while the leaf of the oval lead is thicker in the middle and thinner at the outer edge, preventing it from crimping when it is being bent around curves. You must stretch the lead before using it in order to straighten out any crimps that may have formed in transit and to make it more rigid and easier to work with. It will also lengthen it

Lead is poisonous and can be absorbed through the skin, so before working with it you must either wear rubber gloves (although because they are not very tough they are not ideal) or rub a good-quality barrier cream on your hands.

3. To stretch the lead, place one end of the came into a cleat or clamp attached to the side of your work bench.

4. Hold the other end firmly with a pair of pliers and stretch the lead using a continuous, even tension until it will not comfortably stretch any further. Using the lead knife, remove the damaged ends of the flat lead came by positioning the lead knife vertically across the came's top leaf and applying pressure using a rocking motion. The knife should now cut through the came without crushing the heart or flattening the leaf, thus retaining the original 'H'-section.

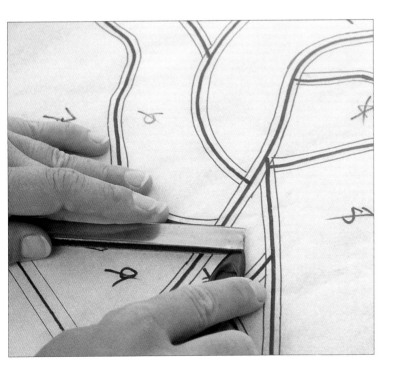

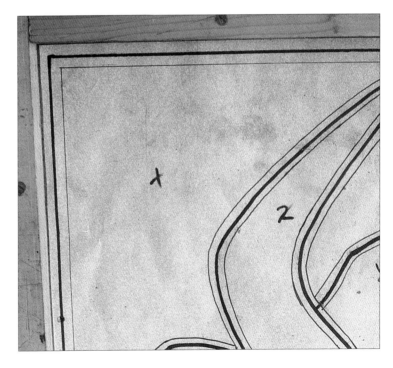

5. You may need to open up the channel again with a fid or oyster knife.

6. Trim off the excess paper on two consecutive sides of your drawing up to the thin, outer line. Position it on the glazing board so that the trimmed corner fits snugly into the right angle made by the battens and stick it down with masking tape. This will act as your guide when you are making the window.

7. Cut a length off the flat lead came to fit the first side of the window panel on the pattern and a second length to fit in the corner at a right angle to it.

8. Fit your first piece of glass into the corner, ensuring that you have seated it securely into the channels of both lead cames. The outer edges of this piece of glass should line up with the thick, black 'heart' line on the drawing.

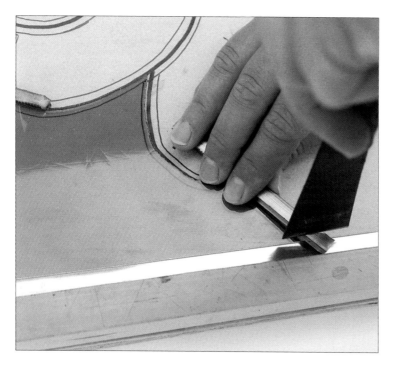

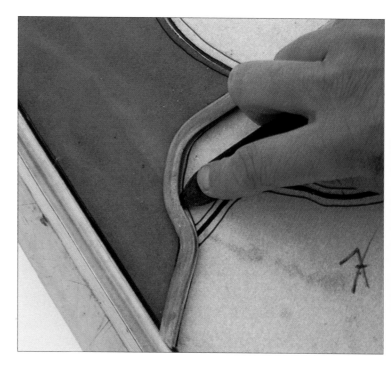

9. Cut a piece of oval lead came slightly longer than that needed for the first lead (marked 1), estimating the angle at which it needs to be cut so that it abuts the edge lead exactly.

10. Ease the came on to the edge of the glass, using a fid to make sure that it has been well seated into all of the indentations.

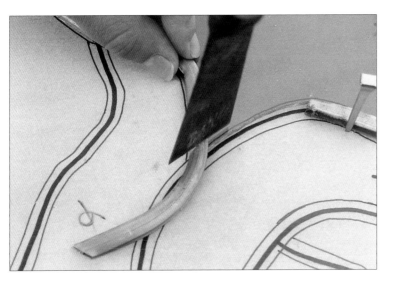

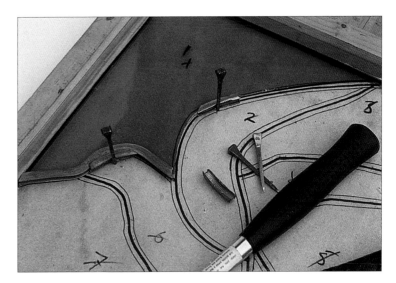

11. Mark where you need to cut the other end by drawing the sharp edge of the lead knife across the surface of the came at the angle required to abut the next piece of lead. You will see from the drawing where this next piece of lead should go, and because the leaf of the next came will overlap the glass slightly, you must cut your first lead slightly short of the edge of the glass. Cut the lead as described previously, using a slight rocking motion.

12. You will need to hammer a horseshoe nail into the base board adjacent to this piece of glass to hold it and its edge lead in position and prevent it from moving. Because the nail is made of steel, it may damage either the edge of the glass, which is brittle, or the lead, which is soft. Create a buffer to prevent this happening by positioning a small lead-came offcut between the nail and the glass or lead.

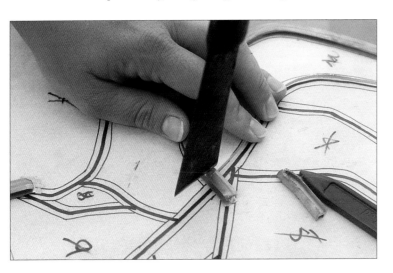

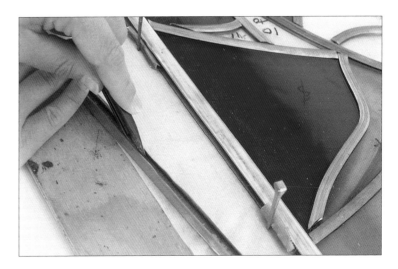

13. Cut a second piece of lead, again slightly longer than required, and trim it at a sharply acute angle where it will abut the other edge lead. Place it securely on the glass, ensuring that it is well seated into the indentation where the wing will fit. Trim the lead slightly so that it will abut its next partner neatly.

The third came will need to be much longer, as it reaches almost from one side of the panel to the other. Take the second piece of glass, the grey wing, and position it in the panel, making sure that it is well seated into the lead cames and hold it in place with a horseshoe nail and lead buffer.

14. Continue in this manner, inserting a piece of glass and then a lead came in the order in which they are numbered, until finished.

When all 12 pieces of glass are in place they should be within the parameters of the drawing. You may need to grind a little off some pieces in order to ensure a close fit, but do not grind the glass before you are sure that this is necessary. All of the outside pieces should now be held in position with horseshoe nails and lead buffers against their open edges. Cut two lengths of flat lead came for the final two sides of the panel. Once the third piece is in place, trim the last one exactly to size. Make sure that the outer edge of the glass is securely seated into the lead came and then secure it with horseshoe nails and lead buffers. Give the nails and buffers an extra-hard tap, as they will need to be very secure when you are soldering the panel.

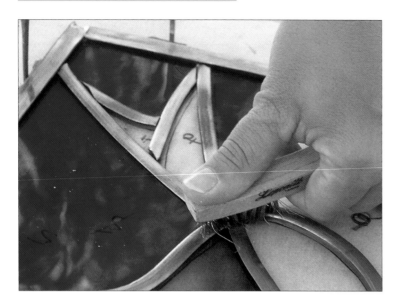

15. Before you solder the joints of the panel, you will need to remove any trace of lead oxide from the cames, otherwise the solder will not adhere to the lead properly. (Although the lead may look very shiny, it will harbour more oxide than is visible to the eye.) Using a brass wire brush (brass, unlike steel, will not scratch the glass), and wearing a dust mask, polish each joint in turn, brushing in two or three different directions, until they are as clean as possible. The only joint that you cannot clean at this point is the inaccessible one in the angle of the two battens.

16. Now flux the joints with a tallow candle to enable them to take the solder, rubbing a generous amount of tallow over each joint. Heat up the soldering iron. Because the melting temperature of lead is very close to that of solder, 50 per cent of solder being lead, it is advisable to solder some practice pieces first to avoid burning holes in the came.

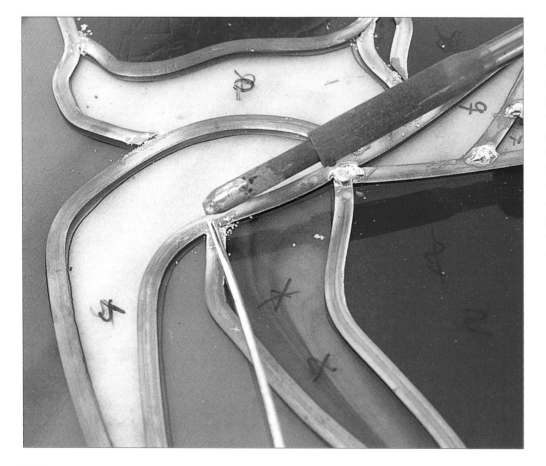

17. When you feel sufficiently confident to start on the panel, solder three corner joints to hold it together. Hold the stick of solder onto the joint and melt off just enough to give a rounded bead that holds the two cames together. If it is not perfect the first time, add a little more flux and try again. Remember not to leave the soldering iron on the joint for too long: it is better to solder the joint twice using a small amount of solder than to try to remove the solder if you have used too much. You may find it necessary to reapply tallow to the joint several times, especially if the lead is not new.

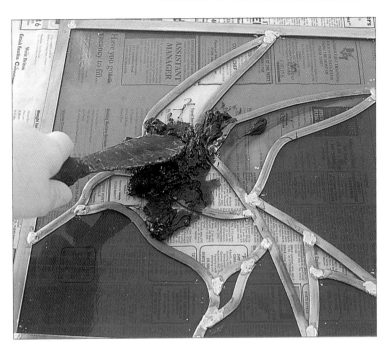

18. Solder all of the joints and then carefully check that you have not missed any. Remove the horseshoe nails and gently pull the panel away from the corner battens. Clean the last corner joint with the wire brush and then finish off this final connection with tallow and solder. Repeat the wire-brushing, fluxing and soldering operations on the reverse side.

19. Although your window is now compete, it is not weatherproof, so all of the gaps between the lead and the glass must be filled with leaded-light cement. (This substance is similar to linseed-oil putty, except that it has a thinner consistency and contains black colouring so that it is not visible beneath the lead in the finished window.)

20. The easiest way to apply the cement is to mix it well, lay dollops of it over your panel and then, using a scrubbing brush or vegetable brush, scrub over the panel, pushing the cement under the leaf of the lead with the bristles and using a circular movement to go around each piece of glass to fill any gaps. Turn the panel over and repeat this procedure.

21. Remove any excess cement from the glass by first sprinkling it with fine sawdust, which will draw the oil from the cement.

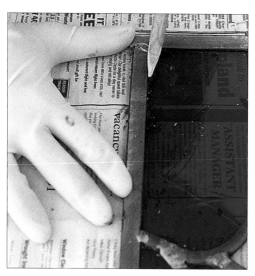

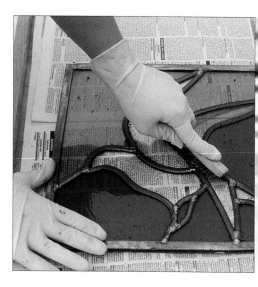

22. Then, with a soft- to medium-bristle brush, and using a circular motion, scrub the window until all of the excess cement has been absorbed by the sawdust. Sweep the sawdust off the window.

23. There will be some excess cement in areas close to the lead. Leave the window to dry for about 24 hours. Then take a sharpened stick or fid and carefully move it around the perimeter of each piece of glass, cutting away any residual cement as you go. This should be 'cheesy' enough to come off without dragging the wet cement from under the leaf of the lead.

24. Go over the panel again with the brass wire brush to remove any cement that may still be stuck to the lead or joints, as well as any residual tallow. Leave the panel to dry for about a week – longer if it's large. Remember that if the panel is moved before the cement has set properly, the seal between the cement and the lead may be broken, making it less weather-proof.

25. To enhance the appearance of the lead, apply grate polish to it with a soft shoe brush. (It is easiest to apply the grate polish to the bristles of the brush before rubbing the brush over the window.)

26. Leave the grate polish to dry for a few minutes and then polish it off with a clean, soft shoe brush.

27. Not only will this give a more professional finish to your work, it will also dull the bright silver of the solder and the parts of the lead that were wire-brushed.

The polish may come off on your hands before it has dried
properly, so leave it for a day or two. If your panel is to be set
into an existing aperture, make it the same size as the glass that is
already in the aperture and then remove the existing glass and
insert it. Secure your new panel with pins and putty, or wood
beading.

Ideas for further projects

Detail of copper tie on saddle bar.

Detail of 'Star of the Sea' window showing traditional glass painting technique.

You are now armed with the knowledge necessary to make any window up to about 50 centimetres (20 inches) high that you care to design. Note that windows larger than this will need extra support in the form of 'saddle bars', bars of lead-covered steel or phosphor-bronze that are set into the surrounding window frame. The panel is literally tied onto these saddle bars with copper wires that have been soldered onto the panel's lead cames before being pulled tight around the saddle bars, and twist-tied. (If you look closely at any church window, you will see saddle bars set all the way up at intervals of 38 to 50 centimetres (15 to 20 inches).)

Traditional stained-glass windows also include details like faces, hands and folds of robes that have been painted onto the coloured glass with special glass paint. This is not the same type of glass paint that we have used in this book, but a shading paint which simply obscures the light. Its main constituents are iron oxide and powdered glass, which are mixed with water and a trace of gum arabic to help the paint temporarily to adhere to the surface of the glass. Once the glass paint has been applied, it is fired in a special kiln to a temperature of 680°C (1,256°F). During the firing process, the powdered glass in the paint melts and permanently fuses the iron oxide to the surface of the stained glass. The technique has remained almost unchanged for at least a thousand years. I have not covered this method of glasspainting in detail, as the cost of the specialised kiln required puts it out of the reach of most hobbyists. From a layout point of view, it is probably more formidable to design a panel using lead lines only, as you are constricted by what is possible to cut in glass.

In this book, I have tried to include projects that range from the very simple to the challenging. They are designed to follow on from each other as your ability improves, so that you need only take a small step at a time.

Most of the ideas can be adapted to suit your imagination and ability. The acid-etched mirrors, for instance, can be customised to make lovely presents for christenings or weddings. If you enlarge the numerals that I have supplied, you could fashion your house number, rather than a name, in glass. In addition, there are many more objects than just boats that would benefit from a stand. And by using glass paints on a drinking goblet, you could make a wonderful night-light holder. The list of possibilities is endless – all you need is a little imagination. I hope that this book will act as a springboard for your creativity, but beware: glass can be an addictive substance!

Glossary

Antique glass: mouthblown, rather than machine-made glass. Not necessarily old glass.

Bead: a line of solder that has been built up until it is rounded and smooth.

Breaking pliers: specialist pliers that meet only at the tip in order to hold and break glass without damaging the edge.

Carborundum stone: a whet stone used for sharpening the lead knife and for taking dangerous edges off cut glass (it must be used wet for this).

Cleat: a device that is clamped to a fixed point, like a workbench, which will grip one end of the lead came when stretching it.

Crimp: to bend the copper foil over the edge of the glass and press it flat.

Cullet: offcuts of glass.

Dalles de verre: slabs of thick stained glass used in some modern windows.

Etching paste: hydrofluoric-acid-based paste that leaves a permanent obscured texture on the glass.

Fid: a small tool used for flattening copper foil onto glass, also for widening the channel of lead came prior to fitting the glass into it.

Finial: a decorative 'button' that screws onto the top of a harp to finish it off and holds a shade steady on a lamp base.

Flash glass: clear glass which has a coloured layer fused onto one side which can be cut through or etched with hydrofluoric acid.

Flux: a liquid or paste substance that cleans oxide off copper or lead and helps the solder to flow more evenly.

Foiler: usually a handheld tool used for applying copper foil to the edges of the glass.

Glazing board: a wooden board, with battens of timber fixed at a right angle in one corner, against which to work when glazing a leaded light.

Grate polish: a proprietary preparation made from oil and graphite used for blackening lead came in a finished window.

Harp: a two-piece structure that fits onto a lamp base, encompasses the bulb and holds the lampshade secure.

Heart: lead came is made in an 'H' section; the heart is the centre bar, which has a channel on each side to take pieces of glass.

Lead-light cement: cement similar to linseed-oil putty, but containing more oil, making it easier to apply. It is coloured black so that it is not noticeable under the lead.

Leaf: the top and bottom sections of lead came, visible in the finished window.

MDF board: medium-density fibre board, a reconstituted board similar to chipboard, but finer grained.

Outline relief: an acrylic paste applied from a tube through a nozzle that acts as a barrier to glass paint.

Patina: a substance, usually copper-sulphate-based, which reacts with solder, causing it to turn a copper or dark colour

Reamy: streaks of colour and texture found in mouthblown antique glass, occasionally reproduced in machine-made glass.

Spider: a small brass ring with three or four prongs attached, which is used for supporting a large lampshade by soldering the prongs into the soldered beads on the inside.

Suncatcher: a small, free-form shape made from stained glass that hangs in a window.

Template: a shape cut from card, used to draw around on opaque glass.

Tessera (plural, tesserae): a piece of glass or stone used for making mosaics.

Tiffany glass: coloured glass which is obscured by the addition of white glass at the making stage.

Tin: to coat copper foil thinly with solder before building up a thicker bead.

Toughened glass: ordinary, machine-made glass, which, once cut to size, is heat-treated to strengthen it. It cannot be cut again, as it would explode into tiny cubes.

Templates

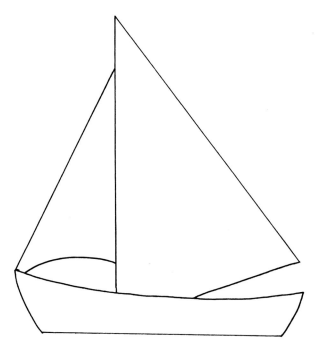

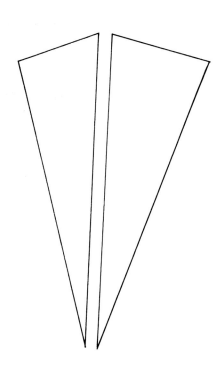

Sailing boat on a stand. Copy or trace and increase by 142%.

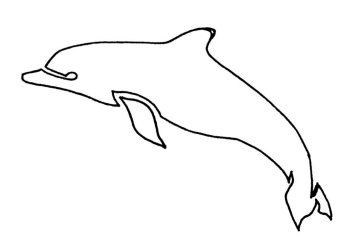

Named mirror tile. Copy or trace and use actual size.

Alternative mirror tile design.

Tiffany style painted lampshade. Copy or trace and increase by 200%.

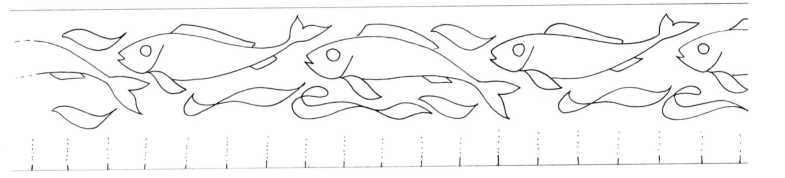

Painted glass bowl. Copy or trace and increase by 200%.

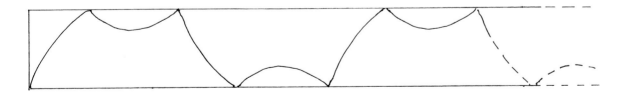

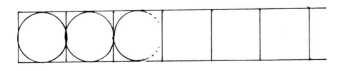

Holly wreath - leaves and berries. Copy or trace and use actual size.

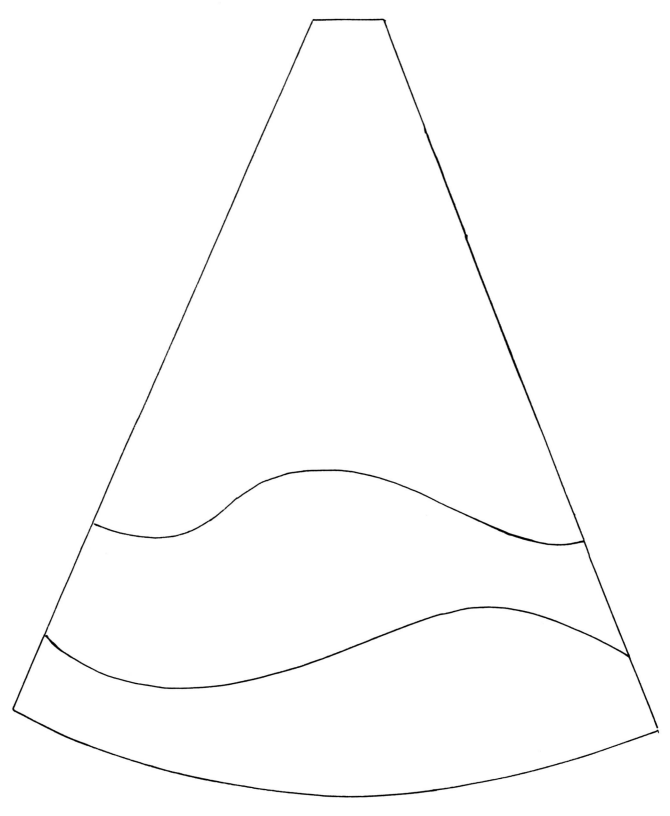

Lampshade. Copy or trace and use actual size.

Greetings card designs. Copy or trace and increase by 142%

Painted roundel. Copy or trace and use actual size.

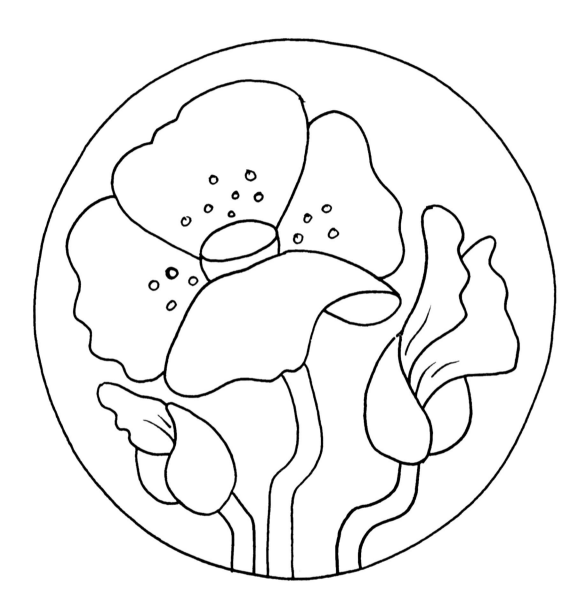

Alteranative painted roundel. Copy or trace and use actual size.

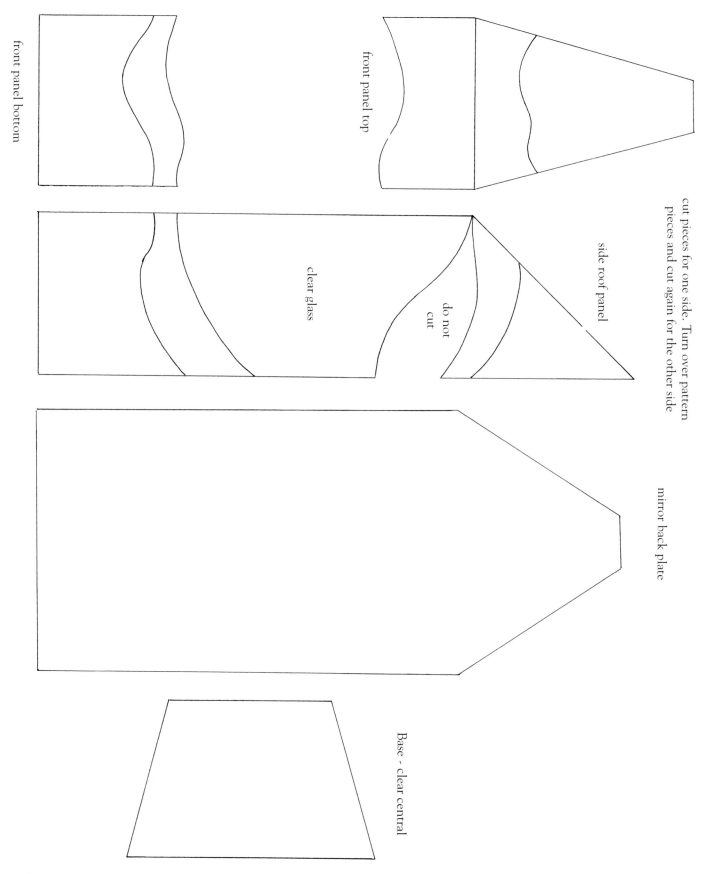

front panel bottom

front panel top

front roof panel

cut pieces for one side. Turn over pattern
pieces and cut again for the other side

side roof panel

do not
cut

clear glass

mirror back plate

Base - clear central

Terrarium. Copy or trace and increase by 200%.

Decorated glass jar. Copy or trace and use actual size.

Index

Suppliers

Fred Aldous
PO Box 135
37 Lever Street
Manchester
M1 1LW
Tel: (0161) 2362477
(Glass paints, glass roundels and small
supplies of stained glass, foil etc.)

Arts & Graphics
4 West End
Redruth
Cornwall
TR15 2RZ
Tel: (01209) 213534 *Fax:* (01209) 211222
(Glass paints, glass roundels etc.)

Carn Metals Ltd
Unit 20
Trewellard Industrial Estate
Pendeen
Penzance
Cornwall
TR19 7TF
Tel: (01736) 787343
(Solder.)

James Hetley & Co Ltd (T W Ide)
Glasshouse Fields
London
E1W 3JA
Tel: (020) 7790 2333/2343 *Fax:* (020)
7790 0201
Mail order, tel: (020) 7780 2346
http://www.hetleys.co.uk
(Stained-glass, lamp fittings and all tools.)

Kansa Craft
The Flour Mill
Wath Road
Elsecar
Barnsley
West Yorkshire
S74 8HW
Tel: (01226) 747424 *Fax:* (01226) 743712
e-mail: stainedglass@kansacraft.co.uk
(Stained glass, lamp fittings and all tools.)

Pearsons Glass Ltd
Maddrell Street
Liverpool
L3 7EH
Tel: (0151) 2071474/2874 *Fax:* (0151)
2074039
e-mail: pearsons@northwest.co.uk
(Stained glass and tools.)

Pearsons Glass Ltd
65 James Watt Place
College Milton
East Kilbride
G74 5HG
Tel: (01355) 230175

Credits and acknowledgements

The author and publisher would like to thank the following people:
Rolande Beugré, Andreya Wharry, Juliet May, Jo Probert, George
and Margaret Teideman, Lewis Hicks, Erica Hicks, Helen Glenn,
Paul Douglas, Michelle Read, and, above all, Sue Lewington.

748.5 HIC
Hicks, Oriel

3000035962

An introduction to stained and
decorative glass

DATE DUE
DATE DE RETOUR